EXIT ON TOP

EXIT
ON TOP

SELL YOUR LAW FIRM TO THE RIGHT PERSON AT THE RIGHT TIME FOR THE RIGHT PRICE

BROOKE LIVELY

Niche Pressworks
Indianapolis, IN

EXIT ON TOP

Published by Niche Pressworks; http://NichePressworks.com
Indianapolis, IN

ISBN-13:
eBook 978-1-962956-16-1
paperback 978-1-962956-17-8
hardback 978-1-962956-18-5

TABLE OF CONTENTS

INTRODUCTION

"CAN YOU COME in here? I think we have a problem. And close the door behind you."

It was never good when my father wanted to talk to me — especially when he wanted the door closed. He had nicknamed me the HBIC (Head B*!#h In Charge) because he knew I didn't shy away from the hard stuff and would tackle any problem lurking in the law firm. On top of those qualities, I was the only business-minded person in an office full of attorneys.

"I'm worried that your brother isn't going to be able to take over the firm. He's a really good litigator, but he doesn't seem to care about anything related to owning a firm."

This wasn't news to me. I had been worrying about it for a while. The succession plan was for Johnathan to take over the firm and for my father to slowly retire. But there were some issues with this plan. Mainly, Johnathan didn't seem concerned about getting new clients, going over the monthly financials with me, or even tracking his billable hours. In fact, he was the very worst in the firm at recording his time. Since I had been thinking about Johnathan and next steps, I had a suggestion for my father, "I think we need to sell the firm."

My father was caught a little off guard. It had never occurred to him to sell, so I explained my thinking. The firm my brother had left to join my father's firm really liked him. The managing partner had made comments to me about how much they also liked my father, and the key comment was how they thought the two firms could work really well together.

After explaining this to my father, I saw some relief on his face.

"That sounds like a great idea," he said. "I'll talk to them tomorrow."

"Whoa, we're not ready to sell — at least not yet," I replied.

All the excitement evaporated as he asked me two key questions:

1. Why not?
2. And how long would it take to be ready?

I quickly answered the first question by listing off a few issues — our marketing wasn't automated or tracked well enough, our profit margins weren't where they should be, and I needed to speed up the amount of work moving through the firm.

As to the second question, he was dismayed to hear, "Two years. And that is *if* people do what I tell them." He waved his hand and said I was the HBIC, so of course they would. I had to explain that while he saw me as the HBIC, everybody else saw me as a PITA.

He asked, "What's a PITA?"

"Pain In The A$$," I replied.

He laughed, and I went off to start the really hard work of overhauling this firm. If we could get it to where I wanted it to be, I knew we could sell and accomplish a number of things:

- Get a cash payout that recognized the hard work my father had put into building the firm.
- Find a partner position for my brother where he could practice the kind of law he loved and not have to worry about firm operations.
- Have a partner position for my father and, more importantly, an office where he could go for as long as he liked.
- Provide a stable home for all the great people my father had assembled over the years.

Knowing what I was working toward and with the support of my father, I started planning how I was going to attack the different issues facing the firm. The challenge was that there wasn't one big thing to fix. Instead, it was a series of small adjustments that would all lead to improving margins and increasing the firm's value.

I found the key to success in the firm's data. Looking at the numbers showed me all the changes (big and small) that needed to be made. We were spending too much on payroll, so I attacked that on multiple fronts. I revamped compensation plans both to better align pay with the goals of the firm and to incentivize the behavior I wanted from each person. Then, I figured out how to streamline operations so that cases moved through the firm faster. Finally, I attacked cash flow. We needed to make it more predictable. I made sure our fee agreements allowed us to charge credit cards, which shortened the amount of time between billing and receiving money to ten days, and I also looked at hourly billing versus contingency work. Again, it was data to the rescue (and a lot of discipline on the part of the attorneys in the firm to stick by the parameters I put in place).

When it came to sales and marketing, I was out of my depth. The firm had always relied on relationships and referrals to deliver clients, and that had worked beautifully. However, I knew that when selling, those relationships weren't transferrable, so they had no value to potential buyers. I hired a consultant who specialized in law firms. That turned out to be the best decision I ever made — not just for my family's firm but for myself as well.

None of this work was easy, and it certainly wasn't fun. While working through these changes, I definitely earned my HBIC nickname. Slowly but surely, I started to see improvements. More work moved through the firm. More clients were coming in from more lead sources. The percentage of revenue being spent on payroll was going down — and this meant profits were going up.

And then I called my father into *my* office and had *him* shut the door behind him.

"Have you ever heard of a TV show called *Love It Or List It*?" I asked.

He looked at me quizzically. HGTV was not one of his favorite channels. I explained the show's premise. Basically, a couple owns a house, and they're given two options and budgets. One budget includes a complete redesign and renovation of their current home. The second budget (which is higher because it includes the sale of their existing house) involves working with a real estate agent to find a new home. The renovation crew tries to create the perfect home while the real estate agent tries to find a new home. The couple has to decide whether they want to love it (and stay in their existing home) or list it (and buy the new one).

"I think we might have been playing *Love It Or List It*," I said.

He still had a quizzical expression on his face.

"Over the past eighteen months, the firm has started running better, and we are taking more money to the bottom line," I added.

He nodded, as he had been happily noting that fact over the past few months. But something else had also been changing.

My brother had gotten married, and all of a sudden, he had started to take an interest in the business side of the firm.

"Daddy, I think we need to Love It — Johnathan seems to. Oh, and there's one more thing. You know that consultant we hired to help with sales and marketing? His clients have been coming to me and asking if I can do for them what I have been doing for you."

When people started approaching me, I realized that it was something I had wanted to do for a long time. As much glory as there was in being the HBIC, I wanted my own business and the opportunity to help more firms than just my family's to achieve their goals. I had stumbled on my calling.

In this book. I'll share my experience improving my family's firm and the expertise I've developed helping hundreds of law firms since then. The book is organized into four parts that provide the details of everything you need to think about as you prepare to sell your firm (or fall in love with it all over again):

- **PART 1** – WHAT DO YOU WANT?
    - Before you can move forward, you need to understand your motivations and where you are headed. This chapter delves into why you are selling and helps you develop a plan for your post-law life.

- **PART 2** – HOW AM I DOING?
    - As an attorney, you want to know every contingency for every situation. To do that, you need to take stock of what is working at your firm and what isn't. Then, you have to educate yourself on the different types of buyers, how they'll look at your firm, and what they value.

- **PART 3** – WHERE DO I START?
    - What constitutes a best-in-class, highly valuable law firm? This section looks at every part of your firm to help you understand where you are, where you could be, and where to focus your efforts.

- **PART 4** – THE SALES PROCESS
    - Selling your firm is a once-in-a-lifetime event, and for attorneys who plan for every possible outcome, the lack of visibility falls somewhere between highly annoying and overwhelming.

Being able to understand the process and know who to rely on creates confidence — which often translates to more money.

If you are wondering if you bought this book too early, you haven't. As you will find, preparing your firm for sale isn't usually a fast process. And if you get it ready to sell and decide not to? Well, then, you have a highly profitable business that runs without you. That's a win-win situation. So let's get started!

WHAT DO YOU WANT?

"**I'M GOING TO** have to fire her."

I couldn't believe I was reading this email, especially since it was before lunch on this employee's first day. This was the second — or maybe third — associate Mike had hired with the idea that she would buy his firm when he retired.

"Can you give her until the end of the week? Or at least until the end of the day?" I emailed back.

I first met Mike a few years before this email exchange. He was running a small firm in a very niche area of law. The firm was doing fine, and he was taking home a nice percentage of the revenue. All in all, he was making about

$230K a year. Not bad when you take all the other factors into consideration — his wife had a high-powered, well-paying job in commercial real estate, they had always lived well below their means, and they didn't have any children, so there was no need to provide for anybody after they were gone. They had saved enough between them to be pretty much okay during retirement. He thought. For the most part. Pretty much.

Then, his wife announced she was retiring in three years when she turned 65. She wanted Mike to retire as well so they could travel and enjoy the fruits of their labors. This put a little more pressure on their savings and pressure on Mike to decide what would happen to his law firm.

At this point, my firm, Cathedral Capital, stepped in, and over the next few years, we walked Mike through the process to help him exit on top. This book can help you do the same. We'll begin by focusing on who you are going to be and what you are going to be able to do once this transaction is over. This is what will carry you through the process, which begins with figuring out what you want.

CHAPTER 1

WHY ARE YOU SELLING?

LIKE MY FATHER, Mike was debating what to do with his firm. In the past, the options were pretty straightforward. You could close the firm; hand it over to a partner, associate, child, or colleague; or, if lucky, sell back your partnership interest. Nowadays, these options have expanded, and attorneys have become savvier businesspeople. However, the initial issue is still the same — is it time to stop practicing law?

People leave the law for a number of reasons, which we will explore in more detail later in the chapter. But the fundamental question you need to answer is, "Are you ready?" This is a question only you can answer, and you are the only one who can make the decision. People who are pressured into selling or retiring are rarely happy.

You must walk into this process willing to explore life beyond the law. This book will help you envision that and see if it is right for you. So, for the moment, let's assume you *are* ready to sell and you *do* want a future outside of practicing law. Now, let's figure out what your motivation is.

KNOW YOUR WHY

As you begin to think about selling, you need to figure out why. A lot of people might read this and think this is a silly question, but it impacts every decision you make going forward in the exit process. Understanding why you are selling determines how you prepare for the sale. Let's look at the most common reasons for selling.

Need Money to Retire

A lot of lawyers are in this category. Their firm has supported them over the years but has not necessarily been profitable enough to allow them to save an adequate amount for retirement. Or maybe as profits grew, so did their lifestyle, and they never prioritized retirement. Now, when it's upon them, they need to do some quick catch-up. And some attorneys love what they do and are always pursuing growth. They may have taken the profits over the years and invested them back into the firm, believing they could make it grow better than the stock market could. In all these instances, a time comes when you want to cash out. Whatever the reason, you need the money to retire.

Want to Do Something Else

Most of the attorneys we work with think of themselves as entrepreneurs who happen to own law firms. As a result, I'm not surprised when they start talking about owning other businesses. Some do it to diversify, some do it to get rid of excess cash, and some do it because, frankly, they are bored. These lawyers have gotten their firm to a place where it runs well and requires very little of their time or brainpower to keep going. The challenge, and therefore the excitement, is gone. So they find something new. Occasionally, they can't do the new thing without selling the current thing — the law firm. It is very common for entrepreneurs to sell part of their existing business to fund a new business — it's just not something we have seen a lot of in the legal world because there hasn't been much of a market for law firms. But as that is changing, I'm seeing more attorneys take advantage of this option.

Ready to Transition to a Family Member

This is what my father wanted to do. Nothing brought him more joy than practicing law with my brother, but he also knew that he needed to set him up for success. Nobody wants to leave a mess behind. But be careful of the magic wand.

One of our clients, Sebastian, was whacked with the wand when his father retired. He came to us not long after he received 40 percent of the $2.5 million firm. His father retained the other 60 percent, with Sebastian having the right of survivorship. Unfortunately, Sebastian found he had a mess on his hands. The lawyers were getting paid too much, and the calculations were more complicated than what it took to get a man to the moon. They were spending a lot on marketing, but he couldn't tell if it was working. And nobody was working as a team — which killed him because he was ex-military and loved being part of a team.

That wand hurt more than Sebastian thought it would! His father hadn't done any of the hard work needed to hand over a smooth-running firm, so it was up to Sebastian to get it done — over the next four years and with our help. And he did. When he "graduated," the firm's revenue was almost $20 million. They were earning a lot more profit and had developed an incredible culture of teamwork and discipline. I recently spoke to Sebastian, and he said they were closing in on reaching $23 million in revenues this year. He had just taken a month off, and his biggest concern was how to transfer the other 60 percent of the firm to himself before his father's death. The firm had gained so much value over the past few years that the estate planning attorneys were worried about how it was going to impact his father's estate taxes were he to die before they figured it out.

Take Care of Your Team and Your Clients

Many lawyers have staff that have been with them for years, and selling can ensure their futures as well. I know firms where the 50-year-old office manager started as a 16-year-old receptionist. The team is fiercely loyal to the firm, and that loyalty is returned. Closing isn't an option. You need to ensure these incredible people, who are talented and great at what they do, continue to be gainfully employed. The same goes for practices that have longstanding clients. Your main concern might be that you want your clients taken care of in the same manner you have always done it, by the people who have always done it. In this case, there is no better way than to find a buyer with similar core values to buy your firm and run it for another generation.

Leave a Legacy

In his book *Fix This Next,* Mike Michalowicz, a business and entrepreneurial guru, created a business hierarchy of needs that talks about legacy in a business as being the creation of permanence, something that will live into perpetuity.[1] Sometimes, this is about the business; sometimes, it is about a name; and sometimes, it is about what you (or your firm) stand for. I think Johnnie Cochran's firm is a great example of this. Mr. Cochran is long gone, but his firm and its values live on. People still contact his firm, believing the attorneys will take on the same types of cases and fight for their clients and causes the same way he did. What they don't realize is that it is now basically a franchise. But the legacy of what that firm did, and what he did, lives on — in perpetuity.

Now, let's get back to Mike and what's next for him. When I first started talking to Mike about exiting his firm, he had to explain his practice area. Frankly, I had never met anybody who operated in such a tiny niche.

---

1 Michalowicz, Mike. *Fix This Next: Make the Vital Change That Will Level Up Your Business.* New York, New York: Portfolio, 2020.

And I mean tiny — very specific. This meant that he was very good at what he did. So good, in fact, that people all over the state of California would seek him out for advice. And he wasn't surprised when he got calls from other states.

Mike's biggest concern was what would happen to his clients if he closed down. He could tell me story after story of clients who had come to him after going to very reputable midsized to large law firms for help. These same clients would then start getting notices from the IRS or the state of California that something had been done incorrectly and they were now in jeopardy. They weren't bad attorneys, he would tell me. They just didn't have the level of deep knowledge he had. And if he shut down his practice, what would happen to all those people? Finding Mike's why was simple. It was right there in what he did every day — helping his clients with his unique expertise. It was his passion.

SUMMARY

What is your why? What are you trying to accomplish by selling your firm? And please be honest, not only with this question but throughout this book. There is no judgment. The goal is for you to exit on top. You are the only one who can define "top." It is different for everybody. And you have too much riding on this process to lie to yourself and others about your motivations or desires.

So be honest — why are you selling?

CHAPTER 2

WHAT ARE YOUR NONNEGOTIABLES?

You can have your price and my terms or
my price and your terms, but you can't have both.

—UNKNOWN (FAMOUS WITH ACQUIRERS)

THE SELLING PROCESS is incredibly personal, and it comes down to one simple fact — everyone defines the success of a sale differently. Mike wants to ensure his clients have the same level of skill and advice he has given them over the years. Mary spells it $ucce$$. Pete wants out — the faster, the better. And Rhonda? She just wants to make sure her name is not taken off the door during her lifetime and that there is always an office where she can go.

The truth is that the measure of success is unique to each of us. It is a multidimensional thing that only you can define, and it is important for you to define it early in the exit process. Your definition of success drives the decisions you make. For this reason, you need to be rock solid in your definition of success so you can identify what things may threaten your success. We call these potential threats to your success nonnegotiables.

For Mike, defining what success meant to him was easy, so we started the nonnegotiables conversation early in our relationship. He believed the discussion would be a short one and started with two nonnegotiables: Find a buyer who had the skill set required to care for his clients and who would keep his existing team employed. Basically, he wanted somebody to simply step into his firm and continue running it.

"Really, Mike? That's all? Price doesn't matter? We can sell it for $100,000?" I asked. That got a pretty good reaction! He answered, "Well, no. They have to pay what it's worth!" During the lead-up to the sales process, I did a couple of valuations for him because his business was rapidly improving, which meant the value was also rising. During this time, I continued to ask Mike about some common nonnegotiables. Many elicited a "not important" response, but a few made him stop and say he needed to think about them more.

"Finding the nonnegotiables is not as cut and dried as I thought it would be," he told me. No, it's not. In fact, it took us months and many conversations to come up with the list that was right for him.

NONNEGOTIABLES AND THE SALE

What things are so important to you that you would walk away from a deal if they weren't included?

What things are so important to you that you would walk away from a deal if they weren't included? There might not be any, but you had better make sure before you sell. Why? Because sellers tend to think a lot about their sale after it happens. And the last thing you want is to end up with regrets. The time to think through your requirements is before, not after, the sale.

Think of it this way. When selling, you are interviewing the potential buyers just as much as they are interviewing your firm. The goal is to find the best match as quickly as possible. Time spent with a potential buyer who doesn't pan out wastes everyone's time and money. So, you need to know what you want out of the deal and be up front about it. This starts with having a great list of nonnegotiables that you can easily articulate.

A friend of mine sold his business last year, and I was fascinated by his experience. He did two things centered around nonnegotiables that I believe enabled him to spend less time on the sales process and feel more confident when it was complete. The first was clearly defining his nonnegotiables, and the second was creating a deal killer letter. And one exercise achieves both goals, so let's get started.

Nonnegotiables fall into five categories:

- Price
- Deal Terms
- Your Team
- The Transition
- Post Sale

Once you have clarity about what you want in each of these areas, you can create what I call the deal killer letter. This is nothing more than a one-page summary of your nonnegotiables. It allows a potential buyer to see if this is a transaction that will work for them or not. For more information about how to write a deal killer letter and to access additional free resources, go to ExitOnTopBook.com.

Price

What is the first nonnegotiable? It is "the number." This is usually the top-line price that somebody is going to pay for your firm. It might be based on the amount you need to retire (if you need money to retire), it might be the amount you need (after taxes) to fund your next business (if you are bored and moving on to something else), or frankly, it might just be a vanity number for bragging rights. Again, no judgment here. Let's be honest so we can get you exactly what you want.

When I asked Mike, I got a wishy-washy answer. For him, selling was not about the number. He didn't want to give the firm away, but he didn't actually need the money. This gave us some flexibility when looking for a buyer that we might not have had if he had been asking for a large payout.

Deal Terms

These are the non-sexy things that are likely to require help from your banker, accountant, money manager, and/ or CFO. Basically, how are you going to get "the number" you decided on above? Are you willing to finance all or part of the deal and have the buyer pay you out over time? If so, how much? At what interest rate? Are you open to having provisions that tie the payout to the firm's future performance — both good and bad?

Another relevant deal term question centers on how much of your firm you are selling. Are you selling all of it, or are you simply allowing a partner to come in? Will they have a controlling interest? If a larger firm is buying your firm, would you be willing to sell your firm in return for stock in the larger combined firm?

And most importantly, whether you are selling part or all of your firm, how long are you willing to work? Most buyers are going to ask for a transition period. While you might want to walk away the day the papers are signed, that is usually unrealistic. But if that is your nonnegotiable, buyers need to know that up front.

As bright as Mike is, his eyes started to glaze over a little bit when I started talking about all these issues. Because money was not his prime motivation, he was willing to finance a large portion of the sale. And because he loves what he does, he was willing to work for up to two years as long as he gained a significant amount of flexibility. Basically, he wanted to dramatically cut his hours, but he was willing to stay on and be very involved for a significant period of time.

Your Team

Some firms have a strong culture with employees who have been with them for decades. These owners generally want to ensure the same firm values continue after the sale. Other firms have a different approach to their team and emphasize things like pay structure and bonus opportunities or the ability to work from home (or not).

As you think about your nonnegotiables, make a list of the specific things that set your firm apart. What makes it unique? What do you want to make sure doesn't get lost in the sale? Think about your core values, benefits, work conditions, and firm culture.

Another important part of your nonnegotiables should be centered on how and when you communicate with your team that you are selling. You need to be aware that this can be a frightening time for your team. The owner they know (and presumably love) is suddenly announcing they are leaving, which leaves the team with a lot of unknowns and uncertainty about your replacement. Selling a firm can be disruptive, so the smoother we can make it with effective communication and consideration, the better.

The last thing to think about is job security. Are there any members of your team who are either integral to operations or whom you want the new owner to guarantee to keep employed for a specific amount of time? If so, you need to be clear about this from the outset.

Transition

A smooth transition involves more than just deciding how long you plan to work after the sale. Before the sale goes through, the buyers are going to conduct some serious due diligence and request to see a lot of information — some of which you might not have. If it requires an outside firm to produce and certify the numbers, who is going to pay this additional cost, and what is the timeline for getting it done?

Once the deal has closed (but you have not necessarily been fully paid), what kind of reporting do you want to see, and how often? Also, during this time, what are you willing to do to help integrate the new owner into the firm? What are the key firm processes that the buyer needs to learn? And how are they going to learn them? Are you willing to educate a buyer on an area of law they might not know?

And the most important transition factor — what is your selling timeline? As mentioned at the beginning of this chapter, *"You can have your price and my terms, or my price and your terms, but you can't have both."* How long are you willing to wait for just the right buyer?

Mike knew he only had as long as Ashley was still working to find a buyer for the firm, so we had a definite timeline. He is passionate about his niche legal area and loves to help attorneys become more fluent in its nuances. Mike felt that bringing the buyer up to speed wasn't going to be a problem as long as they had a base knowledge, were willing to learn, and had the required intellect. The due diligence details he planned to leave to us.

Post Sale

This one is the hardest of all the nonnegotiable sections to complete because sellers have great intentions, but by the time they sell, they are often just done, and they want to be able to walk away. Selling a firm is a long process that requires time, money, and attention. At the end of the sale process, many sellers aren't quite as in love with their firm as they were in the beginning. As a result, the commitments they made on the front end are hard to deliver on the back, which is why it's important to consider specifically what the post-sale timeframe will look like for you.

How involved are you willing to be after the sale? In the transition section, you decided how long you would stay on. Now, you need to take that a step further and determine how involved you will be during that time. Do you want to sit on the management committee? Do you want decision-making authority?

You also need to create a plan that transitions key clients and referral sources. And is there anything specific your firm does that you want to make sure continues after the sale? Do you offer a niche product that might not make a lot of money but serves a purpose in the community? We used to work with a probate litigation firm in Atlanta that carried a certain percentage of their caseload as pro bono work. I know continuing this would be a nonnegotiable for that owner.

Mike was pretty wishy-washy in our nonnegotiables conversation until we got to this post-sale discussion point. Price wasn't a huge deal. Yeah, he was willing to finance a big chunk of the price. Everybody in the office already knew he was selling, so that wasn't an issue. He felt like my team was taking care of due diligence, so as long as we could get the firm sold by the time his wife retired, he was good.

However, he became more passionate when talking about post-sale details because we were talking about his clients and referral sources. These people were important to him and the reason he wasn't just shuttering his firm. He knew these clients needed his specialized knowledge and services. The last thing he wanted to do was to abandon them. This was where his nonnegotiables list started to grow.

Nonnegotiables Process

Defining your nonnegotiables is not an exercise that can be completed in ten minutes or even a day. It takes time and reflection. Spend some time thinking of your own list, write your thoughts down on an index card or a piece of paper, and carry it with you at all times. Take it out multiple times a day and look at it. Are these the right things? What *isn't* on the list that is important? What have you forgotten that, if you don't get it, will create remorse and regrets after the sale? Would you really kill the deal for any item on your list? Deep down, is it that important, or do you just *think* you should kill the deal for it? Don't worry about what other people might think. Nobody will ever know what happens at the negotiation table unless you tell them.

After a few weeks, you'll probably need to rewrite your list. It's going to look a little tattered from use, but hopefully, it will also have things scratched out, added, lines drawn to other words, new words, erasures, creases, and maybe even a couple of holes. If it looks like that, you are definitely doing it right.

SUMMARY

Once you have your list of nonnegotiables, you need to create what we call a deal killer letter. My friend's deal killer letter was awesome and saved him a bunch of time and headaches in the potential-buyer filtering process. He used it to quickly and efficiently eliminate buyers who weren't going to be a good match. Right from the get-go.

> For help getting started on your nonnegotiable list, go to **ExitOnTopBook.com,** where you can access our deal killer exercise, which will help you build your list and write your deal killer letter.

CHAPTER 3

WHAT'S NEXT?

75% of those who exit (their business) "profoundly regret" the decision within 12 months of exiting.

— PRICE WATERHOUSE

WHEN I FIRST stumbled upon this statistic, it was like a punch to my solar plexus. I was stunned, breathless, and slightly panicked. All I could think about were our many clients who were working toward their exits. I hated to think that these owners would sell, and then a huge number of them would regret it. And not just regret it, but PROFOUNDLY regret it.

As a lawyer, your law firm is more than just a business. It's your passion, your identity, and the culmination of years of hard work and dedication. So, when the time comes to sell your firm, it can feel like you're selling a piece of yourself. You may worry about losing control, losing your connection to your clients, and losing the very thing that occupies your time and brings you joy.

These are valid concerns, and they are why it's essential to consider what you're truly selling when you sell your law firm. As I researched, it turns out that the people who regretted selling tended to be the ones who were not mentally prepared for the sale. They didn't understand and plan for what they would be losing. They didn't think about their "what's next."

BIG CHANGES, BUT SLOWLY

When you sell or transition your firm to somebody else, you lose three important things: your "baby," your work identity, and the thing that occupies your time.

Selling Your "Baby"

How many of us have referred to our businesses as our babies or said we were married to them? We started these firms, gave birth to them at a time when they were merely ideas, nursed them through the times when they were sick, and celebrated every milestone, birthday, and achievement. We spent more waking hours with our firms than we did with our actual children. And now, they have grown up to become self-sufficient and are ready to pay us back for all our sacrifices by being sold and funding our next stage of life.

It's a lovely story, but you are still selling your child. Since you started your firm, it has probably consumed more of your time and brain power than your family, and it is about to be gone. If you are not prepared for this large segment of your life to disappear — overnight — you will sit firmly in that 75 percent of owners who "profoundly regret" selling.

What can you do about it? Start taking some time away from the business. Begin with small changes. Take your work email off your phone. When you are out of the office and with your actual family, be one hundred percent present with them. Then, take two weeks of vacation and don't work. You already took your email off your phone, remember? Don't take your laptop. If the office burns down, I promise somebody will call you. But even if it does, there isn't much you can do besides remind them who your insurance company is. Delegate more responsibilities to your team members so you're not as personally invested in the day-to-day operations of the firm. Start to wean yourself away from the office.

Selling Your Identity

Very often, when you go to a party and meet somebody new, the first question is, "What's your name?" followed quickly by, "What do you do?" Right now, that second question is easy to answer, "I own XXXXX Law Firm." Or if you are great at marketing, it might be something like, "I help immigrants achieve the American dream." When you sell your firm, that quick answer is gone.

All of a sudden, your answer becomes, "I used to ..." I used to own a law firm. I used to be an attorney. I used to go to the office every day. I used to solve problems for people. I used to make clients happy. I used to be the head honcho. I used to employ thirty people.

I used to be important.

For many law firm owners, their identity is tied to their firm. It's not just a business — it's who they are. When you sell your firm, you're selling a part of yourself, and it can be difficult to come to terms with that reality.

You may have built a reputation as a trusted advisor or expert in your field, and it can be hard to let go of that status. Your identity may be tied to your clients, your community, or your professional network. Selling your firm can make you feel like you're losing a part of yourself.

But it's important to remember that you are not just your business. You have other roles and identities — as a spouse, a parent, a friend, and more. You can still be a valuable member of your community and profession even if you're no longer a law firm owner.

To prepare for selling your identity, take some time to reflect on what's important to you outside of your business. What are your values? What are your hobbies and interests? What do you want to be known for? By focusing on these things, you can start to build a new identity outside your firm.

It's also important to communicate with your loved ones about the emotional toll that selling your business may take. Share your concerns and fears, and be open to their support and encouragement. Remember that you're not alone. Many business owners go through this process and come out the other side with a renewed sense of purpose.

So, while it may be difficult to let go of your identity as a law firm owner or even a lawyer, it's important to remember that you are more than your business. By preparing yourself emotionally and mentally, you can navigate this transition with grace and confidence and avoid being part of the 75 percent.

So, who are you without your business? What do you like? What don't you like? Practice how you are going to answer the "What do you do?" question. And it can't start with "I used to."

Selling the Thing That Occupies Your Time

Selling the thing that occupies your time can be a challenge for many business owners. For years, your business has been your primary focus, taking up much of your time and energy. It's likely that you have a lot of personal attachment to your work and the people you work with.

When you sell your business, you're not just giving up a source of income. You're also giving up a significant part of your daily routine. Suddenly, you have free time that you didn't have before. You might find yourself feeling lost or even depressed without the structure that your business provided.

To prepare for this transition, it's essential to plan ahead. Think about what you want to do with your free time *before* you sell your business. Do you want to travel, spend time with your family, or pursue a new hobby? Having a plan in place will give you a sense of purpose and help ease the transition.

I love the story I once heard about a guy who was going to sell his business. When asked what he was going to do, he replied, "Next? Build a house in Colorado and retire."

This man thought he had a great plan. The problem was that the plan was only a one-year plan. What was going to happen after that? What was he going to do once he built the house?

Planning a trip around the world or a trip of a lifetime is a one-time activity. When I talk about how you want to spend your time after you sell, I mean day in, day out, and week in, week out for years. Taking a trip or building a house can be part of that, but it's not all of it.

That's why it's also important to stay connected to your community and find ways to give back to the place that has given you so much. Everybody does this differently. For some, it might look like volunteering at the local Bar to help veterans or the indigent with their legal needs. Others might want to serve on nonprofit boards.

Social Connections

The last piece of filling your time is the social aspect. You aren't the only person who has sold your business. Find organizations that have other people like you where you can meet new friends. The Entrepreneurs' Organization is a great group to join and a place where you'll find like-minded entrepreneurs. They might even help you find a new business. You can also seek out friends with whom to play golf or pickleball. And don't forget to keep in touch with your colleagues. You will continue to be a good referral source and mentor for them, and they will be a great source of entertainment for you.

Finally, it's crucial to take care of yourself both physically and mentally during this transition. Exercise, eat well, and take time for self-care. Consider working with a therapist or coach to help you navigate this significant life change.

Some people who sit alone at home get depressed. And if you are depressed, I would guess that you would "profoundly regret" selling your business. So when you take that two-week vacation I mentioned a few pages ago, consider taking it at home. See what you naturally do. Figure out what occupies your time, and develop those interests. Make friends in those areas of interest, and start to prepare for the free time that is coming up.

I felt almost silly bringing this topic up with Mike because I knew exactly what he was going to say. For years, he had been turning down board positions with some of the organizations he loved because he didn't have time to devote to them. Now that he was selling, I knew he would start saying yes. I also knew that he and his wife had a standing Friday night date to go hiking. It was the one nonnegotiable in their marriage. It was their time to connect and decompress, and I knew that with more time, they would be hiking at least three days a week. I also suspected that their travel schedule would pick up. Mike and Ashley usually took one two- to four-week trip a year to somewhere amazing — my favorite was Bhutan. I suspected there would be more big trips, but also some smaller trips to visit their many friends all over the States.

When asked, Mike confirmed all my suspicions. Hiking would move from one night a week to numerous days. He had already been talking to a couple of boards about taking up positions. Ashley had been looking into increasing their "big" trips to two, maybe three, a year, which required a lot of research time from both of them. And Mike was excited about reconnecting with their friends on some shorter trips around the US. I wasn't concerned about Mike being bored, depressed, or regretting his decision to sell. Instead, I was a little concerned about his overly packed schedule!

SUMMARY

You are entering a new time in your life. But unlike when you became a spouse or parent, you aren't adding anything. This time, you are subtracting, and you need to fill the void. You have the opportunity to create a new you — a new identity and a fresh take on who you are. This time, it needs to be purposeful. And if you don't start to discover who you want to be and how you are going to occupy your time *before* you sell the business, you will end up being part of the 75 percent. And that's a majority you never want to join.

CHAPTER 4

WHAT'S YOUR TIMEFRAME?

EVERY SALE IS different, just as every firm is different. And one of the most important sale decisions you have to make is setting your timeline. How long do you have until you want or need to sell your firm? You can take as long as you want, or you can unload it as quickly as you want. But, as with anything else, there is a tradeoff for speed — and it is money. The faster you want to sell, the more it is going to cost you. The more time you have, the more you can improve your firm's operations and increase its value.

When any company goes through a sale, the buyer will always want to see at least three, and sometimes five, years of financials and tax returns. Having this as an anchor point can help you make a decision about what work you want or need to do before you sell. What do those documents look like right now? Would you be proud to show them off or embarrassed?

SHORT TIMEFRAME

I consider a short timeframe to include any sales that have to happen in one to two years. So, if you're thinking about selling your law firm but don't have much time to prepare, you're not alone. Many law firm owners find themselves in this situation, whether it's due to unexpected life events or simply realizing that they're ready to start something new.

The good news is that even with a short timeframe, you can still sell your law firm and get a decent price for it. However, you need to be realistic about the types of improvements and changes you can make in a short amount of time. You most likely won't be able to make any major changes to your firm's operations, so all of its flaws and your past sins will be readily apparent. However, there are some things you can do to improve its appeal to potential buyers. Here are my top three suggestions:

1. **Organize financial and legal documents**. One of the most important things you can do in a short timeframe is gather all of your financial and legal documents and make sure they're organized and up to date. This will save you and potential buyers a lot of time and headaches down the road.

2. **Make a few quick fixes**. Another important step is to identify any quick fixes you can make to improve the physical appearance of your law firm. This could be as simple as a fresh coat of paint or new office furniture. Small changes like that can make a big difference in how potential buyers perceive your law firm.

3. **Set a realistic price.** Finally, it's important to be realistic about the price you can expect to get for your law firm in a short timeframe. You may not be able to hold out for the highest possible price, but with some effort, you should be able to get a fair price that reflects the value of your firm.

Remember the quote from chapter 2 — "You can have your price and my terms or my price and your terms, but you can't have both"? If you are dictating the time (a HUGE term), then the buyers are going to get to dictate the price. Your negotiating position is significantly weakened.

Overall, selling your firm within a short timeframe can be challenging, but it's still possible. Just be realistic about what you can accomplish in the time you have and focus on making your law firm as appealing as possible to potential buyers so you can get a satisfactory price.

MEDIUM TIMEFRAME

A medium timeframe lasts about three years and gives you a bit more time to work on improving your law firm's operations. Of course, you will need to invest more money to make these necessary adjustments. The changes will focus primarily on improving and streamlining your firm's infrastructure. With clients operating within this timeframe, we target two specific areas:

1. **Optimize operations with fractional employees.** Improving operations requires time and expertise,

which makes it a great task to outsource by hiring fractional employees, such as a chief operating officer (COO), chief financial officer (CFO), and/or chief marketing officer (CMO).

Fractional executives are experienced professionals who work part-time for multiple companies, offering their services as needed. This allows you to access their expertise without the expense of a full-time commitment. Plus, these individuals bring a wealth of knowledge and experience to your firm, helping you make the necessary changes to increase its value at a fraction of the cost of a direct hire.

Each of these experts works with you to understand your firm and the next steps. Since they're experts in specific areas, they can help you optimize your firm. Specifically, they'll identify and set strategies to improve existing systems and help your in-house employees execute.

2. **Clarify policies and procedures.** This may not sound particularly interesting, but investing in the creation of clear, detailed policies and procedures is a game changer. Nobody wants to purchase a firm where all the knowledge is housed in the seller's head, especially when the seller is about to depart. Having policies and procedures set up for the firm's operations is essential and should include every aspect of the firm, from marketing and finance to human resources, billing, and, yes, even legal work. Being able to show somebody that the firm can run without you (the owner) invariably pushes the price of the firm upward.

If the documentation task sounds overwhelming, I suggest you read *Process* by Mike Paton and Lisa Gonzalez. This book, part of the Traction Library, was a revelation for me and is certain to help you parse out the process. I'm extremely specific and always felt that procedures needed to be written out with screenshots and instructions that even included arrows that pointed users to the enter button. In fact, Paton explains that documenting 80 percent of a task is all that's necessary.[2]

We all employ intelligent people who can figure out how to hit the enter button. Knowing I can leave the last 20 percent of a process to the users has freed me. In fact, I even wrote a number of marketing procedures that made it much easier to hand off that role to a new member of our management team. Given a three-year timeframe, you should be able to suitably document your procedures, train your team, and ensure that everybody is using them.

Yes, these changes will take time and effort. And both of those things cost money. To get these tasks done, you will also probably need to make some new hires and enlist the services of some consultants or fractional providers.

But, unlike when operating on a short timeframe, you have the opportunity to improve your financials before buyers see them. And better yet, improvements in your firm are likely to result in increased revenue and profit. At

---

2   Patton, Mike, and Lisa Gonzalez. *Process! How Discipline and Consistency Will Set You and Your Business Free.* Dallas, Texas: BenBella Books, Inc., 2022.

the very least, if you can't show ideal financials, you can at least offer positively trending ones.

LONG TIMEFRAME

If you have the luxury of a long timeframe, typically five years or more, you have the greatest opportunity to increase the value of your law firm. This timeframe allows you to make fundamental changes to the structure and operation of your firm and provides the opportunity to put the right people in place to maximize its value. Implementing these strategies and investments enables you to make significant improvements to your firm and, ultimately, obtain a higher sale price.

We focus on the following areas with our long timeframe clients:

1. **Invest in new talent.** A long timeframe gives you the chance to invest in new talent. You may want to hire a chief operating officer (COO) to handle the day-to-day operations of the firm or a chief financial officer (CFO) to manage your finances or a chief marketing officer (CMO) to oversee your marketing strategy. These individuals bring their expertise to the table and can help you grow your firm in ways you may not have considered before.

   In addition, you should focus on developing a strong team of associates and staff members. This means creating a positive work environment, providing training and development opportunities, and offering competitive compensation packages. By investing in your team, you will not only increase the value of your firm but also ensure that it runs smoothly even after you have sold it.

2. **Improve technology and systems.** Another key element of a long timeframe is that it grants you time to improve the firm's technology and systems. This includes upgrading hardware and software, implementing new systems for case management and billing, and utilizing data analytics to identify areas for improvement.

    Investing in technology allows you to streamline your operations, reduce costs, and increase efficiency, which will make your firm more attractive to potential buyers.

3. **Strengthen relationships with clients and referral sources.** Finally, a long timeframe allows you to focus on building strong relationships with clients and referral sources. This means taking the time to develop a personalized approach to clients and referral sources, responding quickly to client communications, yet with a personal touch, so you can continue to build a strong network of referral sources. By prioritizing client relationships, you can increase your firm's reputation and value and attract more potential buyers.

Overall, a long timeframe requires the most from you and your team — the most work and the most willingness to change. It also offers the greatest potential to increase the value of your law firm. It gives you time to fix any operational issues and time to create a high-performing team. This means identifying key positions that need to be filled and possibly considering using fractional services to access their expertise at a much lower cost.

Investing in the right people and systems will not only increase the value of your law firm, but it will also make the transition process smoother for both you and the buyer. You'll be able to demonstrate that your law firm is well-run, profitable, and able to operate effectively without your day-to-day involvement. This is a key factor that buyers consider when evaluating potential acquisitions.

Investing in your firm can provide a double return on your investment. First, the improvements you make will increase the value of your firm when you sell. Second, the changes will optimize operations and are likely to improve profit margins. You will be putting your money right back in your pocket while still working toward your long-term goal of selling.

SUMMARY

Finally, it's important to recognize that a long-term plan requires significant time and effort, and it may not be feasible for everyone. If you're not willing or able to commit to a long-term plan, it may be better to focus on a shorter timeframe or seek alternative options for exiting your law firm. Ultimately, it's about finding the right balance between your goals, capabilities, and resources and creating a plan that works best for you.

When Mike and I originally started working together, we had a medium-term outlook. Ashley, his wife, was going to retire in three to four years, so while we had time to make changes, buyers would see those transitions on his financials. Then Ashley got a call to extend her contract for a very lucrative three more years. This pushed us into the long timeframe, which meant that any financials we showed to potential buyers would show rock-solid, steady revenue and profits. His team was experienced, working effectively, and didn't need a lot of supervision. Best of all, his marketing plan ran almost entirely without him. What we were able to present was a well-established, optimized, profitable firm that was very attractive and could command a high price.

MIKE'S CASE STUDY

Mike's niched practice area, stellar reputation, and willingness to finance the deal made his firm a very attractive acquisition. He struggled early on in the process because he hadn't fully thought through his nonnegotiables, and he hadn't found a broker who could connect him with the right buyers. His long timeframe enabled him to make some significant changes that increased the overall value of the firm and led to a successful exit.

	While Preparing to Sell
Revenue	Increased by 197%
Seller's Discretionary Earnings (SDE)	Increased by 147%
	Sale Price
Multiple of SDE	3.2 with a potential of 4.25+
Timeframe	6 years plus
Type of Buyer	Hire and train a successor

Seller Nonnegotiables:

- Minimum price of 3X SDE
- Buyer must be a core value match
- Buyer must keep the team intact
- Seller not willing to work past 18 months

Types of Buyers Considered:

- Owner Operators or Existing Employees
  - Small firms of 2 to 5 attorneys
  - Hire and train a successor
  - Individual purchaser

What Seller Did to Improve Firm:

- Built the culture of firm so it became an attractive employer
- Made significant investments in systems and data
- Had a marketable firm name not related to seller

Deal Terms:

- Owner-financed with a five-year term
- Fixed payment paid semiannually
- Based on pre-established revenue goals, Seller also receives 6 to 10 percent of revenue paid out semi-annually over same period

PART 2

HOW AM I DOING?

"I'M THINKING ABOUT buying another law firm — in Atlanta."

This was not what I expected Sheryle to say as we were sitting at the gate waiting to board a flight to Mexico for a Mastermind conference with a dozen female owners of multimillion-dollar immigration firms.

"You live in El Paso. Why Atlanta, and why this firm? How did you even find it?" I asked.

"I want to move back to the East Coast, and this firm does a very niche type of immigration law that I would love to get into. And I found it just by googling!" At this point, Sheryle boarded our flight ahead of me.

I spent the next two hours thinking about what she had said. In some ways, I was thrilled. This was a perfect example of a strategic buyer. Sheryle wanted an established firm with a reputation and a trained staff with deep knowledge of this slightly esoteric type of law. On the other hand, she found it on Google. Unfortunately, we were sitting three rows apart, so further interrogation had to wait until we landed.

The story gets even crazier. It turns out that I knew both the firm Sheryle wanted to buy and the broker who was listing the deal. I immediately felt much better because both were very reputable, which meant I could start focusing on the details of what they were offering.

The seller, Irene, had been working on improving her firm for years, which is why I knew her. While never a client, we had moved in the same circles, and I had gotten to know her at conferences while she was trying to learn to be a better business owner.

As Sheryle and I started due diligence on the firm, I could clearly see where Irene had spent her time. She had focused on setting up systems, so her firm basically ran without her, as she was newly married and starting a family. Irene knew that this turnkey efficiency would get her the most bang for her buck as an owner. When Irene had her second child, she decided to be a full-time mom and was ready to sell.

Irene's emphasis on systems served her well when she wanted to sell. The less a firm needs the owner, the higher the value of that firm. During the due diligence process, Sheryle and I only had a couple of questions:

- Since Sheryle lived in El Paso, how much time would she need to spend in Atlanta to run the firm?
- How stable was the team, and would Sheryle have to deal with any staff leaving after the sale?

Basically, we wanted to know how easy it would be to own this firm. And that is the bottom-line question for any sale — How much work will it take to get this firm operating at peak efficiency?

These questions are important for any buyer of a firm — and they're ones that sellers need to be prepared to answer.

What Irene did so well in setting up and growing her firm was anticipating her exit. Everything was built with that in mind. As a seller, you need to evaluate your firm, identify the areas where you are operating from a place of strength (or not), and then start to educate yourself on the different types of buyers and what they want so you can identify who is right for you. This section helps with that process.

CHAPTER 5

GETTING STARTED

IF SHERYLE WAS a buyer who came knocking on your door, could you answer her questions? If not, do you know where you should spend your time to get the most "bang for your buck"?

I'm realistic about how books like these are read. People don't have time to slog through a bunch of information they feel they don't need just to get to a few valuable nuggets.

I designed a quiz that can help you quickly find the information best suited to you and your situation. Each quiz section corresponds to a chapter in the book. Answer the questions honestly, and then, based on your results, you can flip to the appropriate chapters, where you'll learn what best practices look like. If you prefer taking quizzes online, you can go to ExitOnTopBook.com, where you can also learn how improving certain parts of your firm might impact its value.

WHERE ARE YOU NOW QUIZ

Read each question below and circle the answer that most closely matches the position your firm is in today. At the end of each section, add up your score to see how you stack up against best practices. The higher your score, the less work you have to do on that part of your business.

FINANCIAL

What percent of revenue goes to payroll?

<33%	33-44%	45-59%	60%+	I don't know
5	4	3	2	1

What percent of revenue do you spend on marketing?

<5%	5-9%	10-19%	20%+	I don't know
5	4	3	2	1

What percent of revenue is available for you to take home? This includes salary, draws, and expenses you might run through the business.

40%+	25-39%	10-24%	<10%	I don't know
5	4	3	2	1

How often do you review financials?

Each month	Every couple of months	Quarterly	Once or twice a year	My firm can't produce financials
5	4	3	2	1

On a scale of 1-5, how much time do you spend on the financial aspects of your business?

Very little				I spend all my time on the money
5	4	3	2	1

Financial Score: _____ of 25

MARKETING

Where do your clients come from? For example, do they come from referrals, social media, billboards, radio, and/ or pay-per-click marketing? To be considered a source, it needs to produce at least 10% of the firm's leads.

5 or more	4	3	1 or 2	I don't know
5	4	3	2	1

Please answer the following questions on a scale of 1–5 (with 1 being not good and 5 being great):

How complete is your written marketing plan with stated objectives and a feedback loop?

Complete and regularly consulted				I fly by the seat of my pants
5	4	3	2	1

How many of the following metrics do you track, and can you produce? Performance for each marketing campaign, website metrics, lifetime client value, client acquisition cost, and return on investment for each campaign.

They are a valuable decision-making tool				What are metrics?
5	4	3	2	1

How aligned is the firm name, brand, and image with you personally?

I'm not in the marketing				It's "Me Inc."
5	4	3	2	1

On a scale of 1-5, how much effort does it take from you to drive the marketing?

Very Little				I spend all my time marketing
5	4	3	2	1

Marketing Score: _____ of 25

SALES AND INTAKE

Please answer the following questions on a scale of 1-5 (with 1 being not good and 5 being great):

Do you have dedicated salespeople or intake team members?

Yes				No
5	4	3	2	1

Do you have a process for finding and removing friction in your sales and onboarding process?

We have integrated technology				We make notes on a legal pad
5	4	3	2	1

Do you have a training system that includes sales training, software training, and empathy training?

Yes   No

5	4	3	2	1

Do your salespeople or intake team get regular feedback to improve performance?

We listen to recorded calls   I know exactly what I'm saying

5	4	3	2	1

How much effort from you does it take from you to drive sales?

Very Little   I spend all my time on sales

5	4	3	2	1

Sales and Intake Score: _____ of 25

OPERATIONS

Please answer the following questions on a scale of 1–5 (with 1 being not good and 5 being great):

Do you have the right reporting structure in place for your firm?

Yes   I don't know

5	4	3	2	1

Have you documented the processes that cover 80% of the work?

Yes   No

5	4	3	2	1

Does each member of your team own their role?

Yes   No

5	4	3	2	1

Is each member of your team in their ideal role, and are they ideal in the role they are in?

Yes   No

5	4	3	2	1

How much effort does it take from you to drive the day-to-day operations of the firm?

Very Little				I spend all my time in ops
5	4	3	2	1

Operations Score: _____ of 25

PEOPLE

Please answer the following questions on a scale of 1–5 (with 1 being not good and 5 being great):

How deliberate is your firm about its culture?

We talk about it daily				We *might* have core values
5	4	3	2	1

Do you have a documented, repeatable hiring process?

Yes				No
5	4	3	2	1

Do you have a documented operational onboarding and training program with a feedback loop?

Yes   No

5	4	3	2	1

How comprehensive is your career development program for employees?

Everybody
has an   They have
individualized   a job
plan

5	4	3	2	1

How much effort from you does it take to manage your people?

Very   I spend
Little   all my time
                                                             on people

5	4	3	2	1

People Score: _____ of 25

PRODUCTION

How far ahead do you know when you need to make your next billable hire?

6 mos	4 mos	2 mos	1 mo	When I'm buried
5	4	3	2	1

Please answer the following questions on a scale of 1–5 (with 1 being not good and 5 being great):

Does everybody have a billing goal, and are they held accountable?

They see reports each week				No
5	4	3	2	1

Do you know how much work your firm can handle at one time?

Yes				We are slammed or slow
5	4	3	2	1

How confident are you that you have the right ratio of attorneys to non-attorneys?

100%

Not sure
I have
the right
mix now

5	4	3	2	1

How much effort does it take from you to keep work moving through your firm?

Very
Little

I spend
all my
time in
production

5	4	3	2	1

Production Score: _____ of 25

TECHNOLOGY

Please answer the following questions on a scale of 1–5 (with 1 being not good and 5 being great):

How much of your software is in the cloud?

| All | | Firm | | Desktop |
| cloud | | Server | | Edition |

5	4	3	2	1

How well have you implemented your practice management software?

We use 80% functionality				Microsoft Office is working fine
5	4	3	2	1

How well have you implemented your marketing tracking software?

We use 80% functionality				We track on a legal pad
5	4	3	2	1

How integrated is your technology, and how stable is that integration?

Everything is integrated				What is integrated?
5	4	3	2	1

How much of your effort does it take to manage the technology and associated information in your firm?

Very Little				I spend all my time on technology
5	4	3	2	1

Technology Score: _____ **of 25**

If your score was a 25 for any area, congratulations, you are running a best-in-class operation for that function. Alternatively, if you have any 5s, those areas need immediate attention if you want to sell and get a good price for your firm. But it's not as easy as simply working on the lowest score. Buyers don't (and won't) decide on a multiple based on an evenly weighted score. Some parts of the firm carry more significance. Conversely, problems in other areas may be things buyers feel are more easily overcome.

Read on to see how you can use this in-depth understanding of where you are right now to focus your limited time and money and achieve the best possible outcome for your sale.

If you like, you can go to **ExitOnTopBook.com** and see how adjusting your score in the different areas might affect the potential value of your firm.

CHAPTER 6

TYPES OF BUYERS

BEFORE WE GET too far along, it's important to recognize that there are different types of buyers, and each has different motivations and perspectives when it comes to acquiring a law firm. Understanding these perspectives can help you better position your firm for a successful sale and potentially increase its value.

In the current regulated environment, there are three types of acquirers:

- **Owner operators and current attorneys or partners** at the firm who are looking for a profitable business that will bring them financial stability for years to come.

- **Financial buyers** who think they can run your business better and more profitably than you can.

- **Strategic buyers** who are interested in acquiring something that only you have, whether it's your people, marketing, or specific processes. They may also see your business as an opportunity to bring additional sales to their existing firms.

Knowing the motivations and perspectives of these different types of buyers is key to understanding how to approach the sale of your law firm. So, let's dive into each type of acquirer and what they are looking for in a potential acquisition.

Owner Operators and Current Attorneys or Partners

Let's first take a closer look at owner operators and current attorneys or partners. This is the most traditional way to transition a firm, and it can even include passing the business down from generation to generation within a family.

Owner operators and current attorneys or partners are often looking for a profitable and sustainable business that can bring them a steady stream of income over the long term. They are also interested in a business that is easy to run, which means they are likely to see more value in a well-organized and efficient firm.

To maximize the value of your firm for these types of buyers, it is important to optimize all areas of your business, including your financials, processes, and people. The more you can increase the profitability of your firm and streamline your operations, the more valuable your firm will become to potential buyers.

In addition to focusing on financials and operations, it is also important to make sure that your firm has a strong culture and positive reputation. These elements can be key selling points for owner operators and current attorneys or partners who want to maintain a good reputation and build on the success of your firm.

Notice that I am suggesting you look at all aspects of your firm. This type of intensive review takes time, which means that if you are looking to maximize the value of your firm and want to have an owner operator purchase your firm or want to pass it to another attorney within your firm, then you need a long timeframe. This is also going to be the most cash-intensive of all the options for the same reasons. However, owner operator deals have the potential to be not only lucrative but also to be a deal where you can get more of your nonnegotiables than may be available in other deal types.

In short, owner operators and current attorneys or partners are looking for a profitable and sustainable business that is easy to run and has a positive reputation. By focusing on these areas, you can make your firm more attractive to potential buyers in this category.

Financial Buyers

A financial buyer is a type of acquirer who believes they can run your business more profitably than you can. They often come from firms that have been very profitable and run organizations based on systems and processes. These buyers typically have experience running businesses and are skilled at finding and extracting efficiencies.

Financial buyers are very focused on the bottom line and will look for ways to increase profits by cutting costs and streamlining operations. They may not be as concerned with maintaining the culture or core values of your firm as owner operators or current attorneys or partners would be. Instead, they will focus on maximizing profitability and return on investment.

One potential downside to selling your firm to a financial buyer is that they may not see the perceived value in improvements or investments that you have made in your firm. For example, if you have invested in a new marketing strategy or updated technology, a financial buyer may not place a high value on these improvements if they do not immediately translate to increased profitability.

It is important to keep in mind that financial buyers are primarily driven by financial returns and may not share the same values or priorities as the current leadership of your firm. If you are considering selling your firm to a financial buyer, it is important to weigh the potential financial benefits against the potential impact on your firm's culture and values.

Overall, financial buyers can be a good fit if you are looking for a quick sale and are primarily focused on maximizing the financial return on your investment. However, if you are looking for a buyer who will maintain the core values and culture of your firm, you may want to consider other options.

Strategic Buyers

A strategic acquirer is a type of buyer who is interested in acquiring your law firm for a specific reason, such as gaining access to your people, marketing, or specific processes. These buyers are typically larger firms that have the resources to purchase and integrate smaller firms into their existing operations.

For strategic acquirers, the value of your firm lies in the specific elements that they are interested in acquiring. They may not be interested in the rest of your business, as they believe they can come in and run it based on their superior skills in those areas. As a result, they may not place as much value on the overall profitability or efficiency of your firm as owner operators would.

Instead, strategic acquirers are focused on the perceived value of what they are acquiring. They believe it is cheaper to buy your processes, name, skill set, or client list than it is to develop their own. There may only be a marginal return on developing additional areas or skills unless you have developed something else that they specifically need.

In some cases, a strategic acquirer may be buying a complementary business. For example, if they are a larger firm with expertise in a certain area of law, they may be interested in acquiring your firm to expand their services and gain access to your expertise in a complementary area. They may also believe that your clients in a particular practice area might be great clients for them in their practice area. Additionally, they might see a lot of potential in cross-selling services. In this case, it is again cheaper for them to buy your firm than to develop these services on their own.

Knowing that you are attractive to strategic buyers gives you a fair amount of bargaining power — at least where price is concerned. Because they are folding your firm into theirs, you need to find a firm with similar core values because that will not be something they care about maintaining. When you think about improving the value of your firm as an acquisition target, improving that one area where you dominate is the way to up your value. Make sure operations around that skill or area are impeccable. If they are, and you have a longer time horizon, then choose a second area or skill to hone.

Overall, strategic acquirers are looking for specific elements of your firm that they believe will add value to their own operations. By understanding what these buyers are looking for and focusing on developing these areas, you can make your firm more attractive to potential buyers in this category.

SUMMARY

Owner operators are looking for a well-run, profitable firm they can take over and continue to run as a cash cow. If your firm is well-rounded or you have a long timeframe to make adjustments, this is probably the buyer for you.

On the other hand, if you are looking to get out of your high-startup-cost firm, your nonnegotiables don't include worrying about core values, you aren't overly profitable, and your team doesn't have time to make the necessary changes, it is time to romance a financial buyer. They will come in and overhaul your operations in a drive for profitability, so there is no reason for you to expend the energy.

And if you have a firm like Irene's, which is specialized or highly complementary to other practice areas, you are in a position of power. As an attractive target for strategic buyers, you have bargaining power as long as your team's skill set is all it's cracked up to be.

So now that you have a better idea of who might be the right buyer for you today, let's consider what is going to happen in a few years.

CHAPTER 7

DEREGULATION AND BUYERS

LAWYERS HAVE DONE a great job of building a fence around their industry to keep non-licensed people out of the action. However, I believe that era is coming to an end, and in under a decade, we will see non-attorney ownership of law firms. With the deregulation of the legal industry, I expect significant changes in the demand for law firms and an increase in competition within the marketplace.

In a deregulated industry, outside investors will be allowed to own shares in a firm and receive a portion of the profits, which, I expect, will result in law firms becoming attractive investment opportunities. This will lead to a surge of capital flowing into the legal industry, allowing firms to expand and grow more rapidly. It will also lead to consolidation, larger firms, and enormous marketing budgets. Larger operations often have operational efficiency, which drives profits up and prices down and leads to more consolidation. The losers in this are the small law firms.

Does this mean you should sell sooner rather than later? I'm going to use the favorite phrase of all attorneys, "It depends." If you have any kind of personal injury or mass tort practice, competition is going to become fierce, and case acquisition costs will rise. As soon as deregulation happens, it will be a good thing to investigate selling.

And what might this mean for a family law firm? Unfortunately, you aren't as profitable, as sexy, or, frankly, as much like gambling, so many outside investors won't find you as attractive. Hourly practices will feel the impact much later than high-margin or niched practices will.

As more investors and potential buyers enter the market, we should start to see significant increases in the purchase and sale of law firms. The market for law firms will become more robust and dynamic, with more opportunities for mergers and acquisitions.

Moreover, deregulation could lead to greater innovation and technological advancements within the legal industry. Firms could invest in new technologies and processes to improve their efficiency and offer more cost-effective services to clients.

Overall, the deregulation of the legal industry is expected to bring about significant changes in the demand for law firms, the competition within the marketplace, and the investment and acquisition activity in the industry. While it may present new challenges for firms, it also offers exciting opportunities for growth and innovation.

LAW FIRMS AS INVESTMENTS

In a deregulated legal industry, I expect to see an influx of acquirers looking to invest in law firms. Three types of investors are most likely to be interested in this market:

- **Active investors** typically focus on optimizing a firm's operations and profit in order to sell it for a profit in the future.

- **Passive investors** are more interested in acquiring and holding onto a stake in a firm over the long term.

- **Employee Stock Ownership Plans (ESOPs)** allow employees to purchase shares in the firm and have a say in its direction and decision-making.

Each of these investors comes with their own particular approach. Here is a more in-depth review of what buyers might look like in a deregulated environment.

Active Investors

In a deregulated legal industry, active investors (usually private equity firms) will aim to optimize and flip their acquisitions. They are often seen as more ruthless than other types of buyers. They generally believe they can do things better than the existing management team and tend to focus on extracting every possible efficiency they can find, often at the expense of a company's core values.

In many cases, they will not have professional managers in place, which means the existing management team needs to be top-notch to continue running the business effectively. Consequently, when targeting a private equity purchase, sellers should invest the majority of their time and money in developing a stellar management team.

In general, private equity acquirers are more focused on making a quick profit by improving the company's financial metrics. Therefore, if a firm is interested in selling to a private equity acquirer, it should be prepared for significant changes to the business. These buyers are not afraid to make difficult decisions to achieve their goals.

Firms with a short time horizon might be a great fit for an active or private equity buyout, but beware. Private equity buyers are the toughest negotiators out there.

Passive Investors

Passive investors in a deregulated legal industry can take different forms, such as private equity or family offices. These investors want a good return on their investment. Pure investment entities, for instance, are solely interested in the returns on cases settled or won and may not be concerned with the law firm's day-to-day activities. This type of investor can be particularly attracted to practice areas like personal injury and mass torts, where returns tend to be high.

However, it is important for law firms to carefully consider the terms of the investment and the potential impact on the firm's culture and values. Similar to an owner operator, passive investors want a well-operating firm that shows consistent profits. And like private equity, they won't have a professional management team come in and run the firm, so you need to build a strong bench to take over after you leave.

To become attractive to passive investors, it is best to take a holistic approach to your firm, making sure you are strong in all areas. For this reason, a long time horizon and a willingness to invest in improvements will get you the best return.

ESOPs

ESOPs, or employee stock ownership plans, can be a great option for owners of law firms who want to leave a legacy and allow their employees to become owners within certain parameters set by the current owner. This approach can be an effective way to motivate and reward employees while also allowing the owner to borrow money in pretax dollars for a new acquisition.

However, for this to work, the departing owner needs to leave a healthy firm or have a very experienced management team coming in to run it. One issue that needs to be addressed is the potential conflict of interest that may arise when an attorney is both a member of the firm and a trustee of the ESOP. Despite this challenge, ESOPs can be an effective way to create a sense of shared ownership and promote a strong, motivated team culture.

SUMMARY

With deregulation on the horizon, the legal industry is on the cusp of a major change. This shift will result in new types of buyers in the market, including private equity firms, family offices, ESOPs, and passive investors. Each type of buyer has its own advantages and disadvantages, and it is important to carefully consider your nonnegotiables and time horizon before deciding which buyer is best for your firm.

Currently, buyers are limited to law firms and financial buyers, but after deregulation, there will be a wider range of options. Private equity firms can offer significant growth opportunities but may also be more ruthless in their pursuit of efficiency. Family offices may provide a more stable, long-term investment but may not have the same level of financial resources as private equity firms. ESOPs can provide a path to employee ownership and greater employee engagement but may require significant up-front costs. Passive investors may be interested solely in the returns on cases settled or won and may not be as involved in the day-to-day operations of the firm.

Ultimately, when the market becomes deregulated, you'll have more options, but the final decision will remain the same. You'll choose the type of buyer who matches your specific goals and priorities as well as the current market conditions.

It is important to carefully evaluate each option and work with experienced advisors to help guide you through the process of finding the right buyer for your firm. By taking the time to do your due diligence and make an informed decision, you can help ensure the long-term success and sustainability of your legal business.

CHAPTER 8

DISCUSSION OF VALUATIONS

SELLING A LAW firm has fundamentally changed in the past 50 years. Historically, because only licensed attorneys could own a law firm, firms were basically jobs that were handed from insider to insider, used to accumulate as much savings as possible before shutting down or being passed to another insider. They had no value on the open market, so little value in a sale.

Very often, lawyers took what I call the magic wand approach. They would wave a magic wand and magically gift over all or part of their firm to another person. Firms are now recognized to have intrinsic value, and the IRS recently started requiring firms to disclose partnership interests. Both of these facts mean that gifting stock in a firm can have tax consequences. Please be wary of this very traditional option and contact a tax professional before taking this path.

As I write this book, Arizona and Utah have allowed non-attorney ownership of law firms. Utah has its own sandbox, and Arizona is doing it through Alternative Business Structures (ABS). The accounting and dental industries have already gone through deregulation, and we can learn from their process. We *will* see the consolidation of firms with a drive for more efficiency. I am already seeing more firms change hands than ever before. This means that a market is developing in which to sell your firm — which is great news for you.

But the big question remains, "How do I value a firm?" The reason we are talking about it now is that it hinges on two things:

1. What parts of your firm operate well (and which don't)?
2. What type of buyer are you attracting?

These two factors impact the price that will be paid for your firm.

It's time to dive into the nerdy world of valuations. Now, I know what you're thinking, "Ugh, math. No thanks." But hear me out because understanding how your firm is valued is crucial to getting the most out of a sale. There are three main ways professionals value a company: book value, the discounted cash flow method, and comparative analysis (with its subset, multiples).

Book Value

First up, let's talk about book value. This is the valuation number you hear about all the time on television and financial shows. It is the simplest way to value your firm because it is a simple math formula: your company's assets minus its liabilities. Basically, you add up everything your company owns and subtract what it owes, and voila, you have your book value.

But here's the thing. Book value is not a great way to determine the sale price of your firm. Why? First, law firms don't own what we call fixed assets. You don't have expensive machinery (no, those computers you bought five years ago aren't worth much), and a well-run law firm doesn't have significant accounts receivable. In addition, book value doesn't take into account intangible assets, like your firm's reputation, client base, and brand recognition.

Discounted Cash Flow

The second valuation method is discounted cash flow (DCF). This method is a bit more complicated, but it's considered one of the most accurate ways to value a business. All the finance geeks (including myself) love this one. The basic idea is that you project your firm's future cash flow and then discount it to its present value. The key to getting this right is making accurate projections. It's important to consider things like market trends, competition, and potential risks.

You also need to calculate the discount rate by adding a risk premium" to the 10 Year Treasury Rate. And the risk premium is where a number of judgment calls come into play, especially when looking at company-specific risk. Anyone doing a valuation decides (on a scale of 1-10) how risky your projected revenue growth is, how much operational risk your firm has, whether too much of your revenue is concentrated in too few clients, where your competitive position is, and the quality of your management team and staff. On top of that, they add more judgment calls and then decide how to weigh all those judgment calls.

Now that your eyes have glazed over and you are checking to see how long this section is, I'll add a story to make it more interesting and pertinent. When I was in grad school, I noticed that by changing the risk premium (and therefore the discount rate), I could *wildly* affect the price of a stock. I called a finance friend who had recently retired from Goldman Sachs to figure out what was happening, and he just started maniacally laughing. I think there was still a little PTSD there. He was on the Goldman team that took the Chinese state-owned oil company Sinopec public. When my friend and his coworkers arrived in Beijing on day one, they were basically told what the valuation number should be by the Chinese government. By adjusting the risk premium, they were able to make that happen.

So what does that mean for you? Basically, if a seller is using a DCF model to price, they are going to push the risk premium down and have very optimistic growth projections, both of which will push up the value. The buyer's valuation people will do the exact opposite, pushing the value down. Ultimately, you hit a stalemate. This complicated process doesn't necessarily reflect the realities of law firms since the risk premium questions aren't truly geared for legal entities.

Comparative Analysis and Multiples

The third method for determining valuations involves comparative analysis and multiples. A comparative analysis compares like things and is a great way to value service-based businesses because you look at all kinds of different attributes (multiples) and then compare only the truly similar items. For instance, you can compare the sale prices of firms that are the same size, in the same practice area, and/or located in the same city or state.

A multiple is basically a number that you multiply your firm's earnings by to get its valuation. For example, if your firm has earnings of $1 million and the multiple is 5X, then your firm's valuation would be $5 million. The hardest part of the multiple process is finding similar firms that have sold so you can see what multiple the market is willing to pay.

So, what is the average multiple for law firms? According to Tom Lenfestey at The Law Practice Exchange, who has probably been involved in the sale of more law firms than anybody else in the US, the average multiple ranges from 2.5X for typical small firms to breaking 4X for proven firms with consistent revenues that don't rely on the owner.[3]

And what impacts your multiple? To some extent, it is driven by the type of buyer you have and what they want. Sheryle wanted a specific location (East Coast), niche practice area, well-trained staff, strong firm reputation, and online marketing that reliably produced cases. An owner operator will also care about location and practice area, though they might be more willing to develop the reputation or staff.

---

3   Tom Lenfestey, interview by Brooke Lively, 2023.

One surprising finding is that a strong sales department is usually not that highly valued. Yes, you read that right. Sales, which are the lifeblood of your firm, are not the most important factor when it comes to valuing your firm.

What Adds Value?

So, what adds the most value? It's a combination of things, really. A strong brand, a loyal client base, a talented team, a firm that doesn't need a lot of time or effort from the owner, and a solid track record of profitability — these all contribute to a higher valuation. But at the end of the day, it's still a judgment call on a multiple. That's why it's important to work with an experienced advisor who can help you navigate the valuation process and get the most out of your sale.

I was doing a valuation a few years ago and called a friend from grad school who does general valuations all day, every day, for a living. I asked him if he could pull some law firm sale comps for me, and he said sure. He called back a little later and said he wasn't sure how much help he could really be — there were only two reported law firm sales in his database over a multiyear period. This is changing, and I expect it to improve as more attorneys realize their firms are an asset and they decide to sell. I also believe that deregulation will cause more firms to change hands. In the meantime, companies like Lenfestey's Law Practice Exchange are valuable. As a leader in helping attorneys buy and sell firms, it is an incredible repository of multiples and comparable information.

This is exactly where Sheryle found herself — working with The Law Practice Exchange. They looked at Irene's firm, agreed on a multiple based on the way the firm operated, and then made a few price adjustments because of the way the firm billed and collected. The method was simple, clean, transparent, and effective.

SUMMARY

There are a lot of nerdy ways to find the sale price of your firm, but it will most likely come down to a judgment call on a multiple. Book value is a simple but flawed method, and discounted cash flow is accurate but requires careful projections. Multiples reflect what is going on in the market. Ultimately, what adds the most value is a combination of factors, including a strong brand, loyal clients, a talented team, and a solid track record of profitability. So don't be afraid to get nerdy with valuations, and remember to work with an experienced advisor to help you get the most out of your sale.

Do you want to find out more about the value of your firm? Go to **ExitOnTopBook.com** and use our free tools.

CHAPTER 9

PSYCHOLOGY OF FIXING

FOR MOST SELLERS, the first time they are told the value of their firm, it is below what they want to hear. The natural next question is something like, "What do I have to do to get $X?" As always, there are options.

Debt reduction is one way to improve a firm's value. When somebody decides to get rid of all their debt, they have a few strategies to choose from, each with its own perks.

Let's start with the **snowball method**. It's all about building momentum: pay off your smallest debt first while making minimum payments on the rest. Once the smallest debt bites the dust, roll that payment into tackling the next smallest. Keep rolling, and eventually, they are all paid off. It's a great way to knock out some quick wins and stay motivated.

Now, if you're more of a numbers person, consider the **avalanche method**. With this strategy, you pay off the debt with the highest interest rate first, which saves you money in the long run. Once that's paid off, move on to the debt with the next highest interest rate, all the while making minimum payments on everything else.

Why am I talking about paying off debt? Because now that you have evaluated your firm and know where your strengths and weaknesses are, you need to decide what you are going to work on and in which order. To effectively prioritize, you need to consider five different things: timeframe, buyer, personality, skill set, and value creation.

Timeframe

Part of your decision on what to fix first is driven by your timeline. If you are selling right now, there's not much you can do. Put as much lipstick on that pig as possible and accept your fate. But if you have more time, you also have more options.

Buyers

Another consideration is the type of buyer for your firm. If you want to be acquired by private equity, concentrate less on making the financials and processes work. These are areas where private equity buyers will want to come in and overhaul it themselves — with their key skill being operations. You want to focus on what they don't have time to do, which is to create an effective management team.

Personality

Believe it or not, your personality will impact what area of business you tackle first. What is your personality? Are you a lowest-balance-first person who needs a quick win? Then look at your firm and figure out where that will be. There is nothing worse for somebody with your personality than slogging through and seeing no progress for a long time. What is one area where you can make a few changes that will have a big impact? Attack that first, reassess, and then choose the one that seems easiest for round two. Continue doing this until you are running a best-in-class firm or you sell — whichever comes first.

Assess the personality and strength of your team as well. Hopefully, you've built a group with skills that differ from, yet complement, both yours and each team member's. How do they work best? Some teams are able to take on a lot of projects at once, and the upheaval caused by this change doesn't affect the team's overall performance. In most cases, that doesn't happen, and a more methodical approach is the order of the day.

Go back to the quiz. Pay special attention to areas where you gave yourself low scores on the amount of time and effort a particular area of your firm required from you. The new owner is going to have to spend the same amount of time and effort, if not more, once they buy the firm. This can be a big hurdle in a purchase, especially if it is a second firm like Sheryle's. One of the things she really needed was an owner who had removed herself from most of the firm's day-to-day management. Without that element, there was no way she could run it from El Paso. How can you remove yourself from the firm?

Skill Set

And more than anything, you need to be brutally honest. When I was studying for the CFA exam, I had a hard time with a specific section. It didn't seem to matter how hard I studied or how many review courses I took. I failed that section on every practice exam. I happened to know the man who founded the premier review course (think BARBRI but for CFAs), and his advice was simply to walk away from that section. I thought he had lost his mind. But we did the math, and I could still pass if I failed that section.

The same might be true for you and your team. One area might be beyond your skill set and your ability to fix, change, or evolve in the required amount of time. Trying to make this change would do nothing but demoralize the team.

You have to know when to walk away.

Value Creation

However, if you decide to walk away because your team doesn't have the skill set, that does not mean your firm needs to walk away from selling. There are experts who specialize in helping law firms optimize every aspect of their practice. Professionals with expertise in specific areas can move your firm forward significantly faster than you could on your own. The question is, how much does it cost, and can you afford it?

I want to add one more facet to these calculations. Firm owners are great at calculating how expenses will affect the profit of their firm. And often, what they see — especially in the short term — is that their personal income will go down. What I want you to calculate is the value that professionals can create.

Value is determined by multiplying net operating income (the profit number *before* you run all your personal expenses through the firm) by your anticipated sales multiple. Remember, the multiple range is 2.5X for the average small firm, 3.5X for an upper-band dominant firm, and 4X+ for best-in-class firms with a proven record of consistent revenue and high profits that don't require a lot of effort from the owner.

I want to work through an example of hiring somebody to help you fix a part of your firm. Let's say you hire a fractional CFO to help you improve your margins.

Before	
Revenue	$100
Payroll	$(40)
Marketing	$(13)
Overhead	$(31)
NOI	$16

After	
Revenue	$100
Payroll	$(35)
Marketing	$(9)
Overhead	$(26)
NOI	$30

If you anticipate having a 3.5X multiple, your firm value before hiring a fractional CFO was $56. Afterward, it is $105. Okay, so 49 dollars doesn't sound like a whole lot. But what if you are doing $2.5 million in revenue?

Before	
Revenue	$2,500,000
Payroll	$(1,000,000)
Marketing	$(325,000)
Overhead	$(775,000)
NOI	$400,000
Value	$1,400,000

After	
Revenue	$2,500,000
Payroll	$(875,000)
Marketing	$(225,000)
Overhead	$(650,000)
NOI	$750,000
Value	$2,625,000

Would it be worth hiring that fractional CFO company now? How much would you be willing to pay to have the value of your firm almost double? Not to mention that the same increase will happen to your income while you are waiting to sell.

Go back to your quiz scores and think about them again using the five criteria listed below.

- **Timeframe:** How much time do you have?

- **Buyer:** Who is your ideal buyer, and what will *they* value? And almost as important, what will they *not* value?

- **Personality:** What is the personality of your team? Do you need a quick win and need to take on an easy project first, or can you attack a longer project that might have a bigger impact?

- **Skill Set:** What skill sets do you have in-house, and what, if any, do you need or are you willing to hire on a fractional or project basis?

- **Value Creation:** Most important, where can you create the most value?

Make a list answering these questions. Which things will take your multiple from 2.5X to 4X? Put in dollar values where you can. Discuss with your team. Prioritize. Talk to outside providers. Reevaluate and create a plan with achievable milestones that you can start working on ASAP — because every dollar of your net operating income matters.

SUMMARY

It is possible to positively impact the value of a firm by pulling one or more of five levers: timeframe, buyer type, your (and your team's) personality, your and your team's skill set, and your willingness to pay for value creation. Not every seller has the luxury of time, but they may have a highly skilled team. Go back to the quiz, look at where your strengths and weaknesses are, and evaluate, based on your resources of time, money, and skills, how to best improve your answers.

SHERYLE'S CASE STUDY

Sheryle was a strategic buyer with cash, time, and the ability to jump on the right opportunity. What made Irene's firm attractive was its niche and complementary practice area, the fact that it was systems-focused (so it took very little time from the owner), and it was in a geographically desirable area. The stars aligned. Sheryle was ready to purchase, and Irene had built the firm to sell.

	At Time of Sale
Revenue	$2.4MM
Sale Price	$975K
Multiple of SDE	3.1
Timeframe	10 years since firm inception
Type of Buyer	Strategic Buyer

Buyer Nonnegotiables:

- East Coast location
- Niched practice with stable team
- Practice that runs with little oversight
- Core value match

What Increased the Multiple:

- Highly trained staff in a niche area of the law
- Seller made a significant investment in systems so the firm would run efficiently without her day-to-day oversight — especially important since she had married and had two children while building the firm

What Decreased the Multiple:

- Firm had the seller's name and image embedded in the firm name, URL, and all branding
- Firm was well below ideal profitability ratios

Deal Terms:

- Cash offer to seller
- Buyer used mix of cash reserves and an SBA loan
- Seller stayed on in a part-time role for six months to transition clients and referral sources and to teach the buyer the specific area of law

PART **3**

WHERE DO I START?

"**LET ME GRAB** my credit card from the car, and then can we start on the first of the month?" asked Sebastian.

"Uuummm, sure," I replied, a little taken aback by the speed with which he had made the decision. While he grabbed his card, I spent those quick couple of minutes trying to figure out exactly what had just happened.

When Sebastian got back, I said, "You know, you have the dubious honor of being my quickest sales call — ever. We had an hour scheduled for this, and we still have forty-five minutes left. Is there anything else you want to work on today?"

Sebastian started working for his father when he entered practice, and over time, he was gifted 40 percent of the firm. By the time we met, he had taken over the day-to-day operations but had been stuck at $5.5 million in revenue for about three years. He was frustrated. For an action-oriented guy, this kind of stagnation was, frankly, unacceptable.

What I encountered in that conversation continued throughout our relationship. On that call, I saw what would prove to be Sebastian's "secret sauce" — his execution skills.

He executed. Consistently. Was it always the right decision? No. But, he and his team started making fast decisions based on data and executed them quickly and efficiently. And it paid off.

He graduated from Cathcap about four years later, when he brought the financial brain trust in-house, having grown the firm to about $20 million. And this year, he will do $24 to 25 million.

We loved being part of the team that helped him achieve that growth and the associated profit. And yet, it created an unanticipated set of problems. Remember that 60 percent that his father still owns? Early this year, Sebastian got a call from his father's estate attorney, who was concerned that if his perfectly healthy and active father didn't die before the inheritance laws change in a couple of years or if they couldn't figure a way to legally (and fairly) transfer the rest of the firm to Sebastian, the family would be stuck with a huge estate tax bill. Sebastian had increased the profits and value of the firm so much that he pushed his father into a whole different tax stratosphere.

In this section, we are going to look at the different parts of your business that can impact the valuation and attractiveness of your firm. The goal is to achieve best-in-class in as many places as possible based on your team and timeline. And I'm going to use Sebastian as an example of how execution in different parts of your firm can impact its value.

CHAPTER 10

FINANCIALS

I STARTED MY career as a financial person, and financial analysis is the focus of my company. So, of course, I believe that financials are the most important part of selling your law firm. But the truth is, the financials are nothing more than a scorecard or report card that reflects the operations of your firm. Let's start by discussing this scorecard because it tells us everything we need to know about your firm and everything a potential buyer is going to look for.

Financials are backward-looking documents that tell how a business performed. Did it make money, lose money, spend wisely, spend foolishly, not have the means to make money, or have too many people on payroll to have a chance of profit? It holds the key to what is actually happening at a business, and this is important.

In the chapter about selling timeframes, I talk about how long you have to get your firm ready to sell and explain why the longer the horizon you have, the better. And that is because, very often, firms need to overcome evidence of poor management that shows up on their financial statements. Since buyers will want at least three years of financials, a longer sell timeframe gives you a better chance of making sure those are solid numbers.

WHAT BUYERS LOOK FOR

What does a buyer want to see? First, they want complete financials. You can easily produce the documents they ask for without any holdup or drama. In most systems, a profit and loss statement and a balance sheet can be generated in less than three minutes. This information gives buyers confidence that you are not manipulating numbers and have nothing to hide.

Then, potential buyers are going to start to dig a little deeper to see *how* the books are kept. Are they clean? Does everything balance? Or is your bookkeeper going in at the end of the month and making what are called journal entries (or plug entries) to make things balance? That is sloppy work, and it causes buyers to dig even deeper, as it is usually a sign that there might be more bad things happening, which they'll find if they look a little harder.

Buyers also want to read the financials to hear the story they tell about the firm. After glancing at your top-line revenue number, the first thing they will do is look at the bottom line to see how much profit you had. They want to see a healthy number approaching 30 percent.

They are then likely to start looking at payroll. How much is it costing the firm to generate that top-line revenue? When you add up salaries, taxes, and benefits, this number should also be hovering at about one-third.

But there is a caveat to payroll spending. As a firm grows, it starts to hire people who are not directly involved in billing that top-line revenue number. At some point, after you cross the seven-figure mark, the owner spends less time practicing law and more time being the CEO of the firm. That CEO salary should be divided, with a portion added to attorney salaries and the rest put in overhead salaries. The portion allocated to overhead should be for people like the bookkeeper, the on-staff IT guy, and the office manager.

When I discuss salaries for the marketing and sales teams, the question quickly comes up: Where do their salaries belong? They go in the marketing section, which is a subsection of overhead. Marketing should be no more than 10 percent of revenue. This means that for every dollar you spend on marketing — and this includes an in-house marketing team member, a salesperson, and/or a pay-per-click campaign — you should get, on average, ten back.

TOTAL OWNER COMPENSATION

The ultimate financial number any buyer cares about is what we call total owner comp or what a lot of merger and acquisition guys call SDE (seller's discretionary earnings). You get this number by combining a few numbers that are found in multiple places. If you present them clearly to the buyer, you can earn a few brownie points.

SDE represents the entire benefit you get from your firm. It is the sum of your firm's net profit, your salary, the taxes on your salary, the value of all your benefits, and any personal expenses you run through the firm. Frankly, I don't care if you run stuff through the firm — that is between you, your accountant, and the IRS. What I do care about is showing these things to the buyer because they don't have to spend that money. It makes your firm appear more profitable and, therefore, more valuable. So please, fess up to anything and everything you might run through the firm. Even that five-dollars-per-month *Wall Street Journal* subscription. It adds up. Stripping out these expenses is called "normalizing" the earnings.

When we work with firms, we generally reorganize their profit and loss statement so that it shows all these expenses in one place. This accomplishes two things. First, if the firm sells, it takes us minutes to normalize the earnings. Second, most owners don't realize the true amount they benefit from their firm. We believe that seeing that benefit in one place boosts the morale of our owners. They realize they are being paid more than they thought for the time, effort, and risk they are taking in owning their firm — and displaying their financials in this way doesn't affect their taxes.

Sebastian was surprised the first time we did this for him. He realized that he wasn't making what he thought he was. He was making more! And as he grew his firm, he monitored that SDE number and was willing to let it dip in his quest for growth. In the short term, Sebastian would give up some of his total owner comp or SDE, knowing that, in the long term, it would increase the value of his firm and his future earning potential.

SUMMARY

As you prepare to sell, you want to increase and harvest as much profit as possible. Basically, you want to do everything you can to boost your SDE or total owner comp. Once you can show a solid three- to five-year track record (or at least a steady upward trend for that amount of time), you are ready to shop your firm. But remember, if your financials aren't clean, there will be a lot of skepticism about their accuracy, which will depress the value of the firm. And if you don't have a solid history of profitability, that will also lower the sale price.

If you don't know what your total owner compensation or SDE is, go to **ExitOnTopBook.com** for resources to help you calculate it.

CHAPTER 11

MARKETING

IF YOU ARE an acquisition target, the acquirer is looking for two things: Do you have a brand that can be transitioned, and do you have a best-in-class marketing department? Marketing is an essential component of any successful law firm. It's not just about getting the word out about your services; it's about creating a brand that aligns with your mission, vision, and values.

A best-in-class marketing department has a clear plan of action, with stated, anticipated results that align with the goals of the firm. As you consider selling your firm, a buyer is going to want to see evidence that this is in place — and operating without the intervention or efforts of the current owner.

TRANSFERABLE BRAND

Does the firm have a brand separate from the personality of the current owner?

Think of it this way. Say your firm is named John Smith, PLLC. All the marketing features your (John Smith's) image, and your website is JohnSmith.com. Unless you find some other guy named John Smith who happens to look exactly like you, it is going to be really hard to sell your firm. Why? Because you built your firm on your personal brand. And it is very hard to sell yourself.

If you are thinking about selling your firm, and it is named after you, you need to immediately start thinking about what a brand refresh would look like. What would a new name look like? What about Legal Eagles PLLC? Even if your state prohibits the use of trade names, see if you can at least add more names to diminish the reliance on just one personality. And for heaven's sake, put the word Associates in there![4]

A name change requires many additional follow-on adjustments. You will need a new URL and a refresh of the website content to highlight the team as opposed to the founder. (Because, remember, we can't sell the founder!) Does the content still speak to the expertise of the firm and the value you all bring? Does it demonstrate that you are a game changer in your practice area?

The final and arguably most important part of the process involves reviewing the firm's mission, vision, and values. Do these continue to align with the new brand, or do they need to be adjusted? Were these things focused on you (the soon-to-be departing founder) and now need to be redirected to reflect the longevity of the firm? You need to

---

4   There are still some states that prohibit the use of trade names. At the time of writing, these include New York, New Jersey, Ohio, Illinois, South Carolina, Tennessee, and Virginia. But check your Bar rules; those rules are changing.

create a brand that will outlive you as the founder and be attractive to potential buyers as well as existing and potential employees. When you have a great team, you attract wonderful clients.

Sebastian's firm carries his family's name, and he recognized that as a problem. Over the years, he slowly bought and built out URLs that complemented his practice areas. They align with the overall brand of his firm yet are beginning to dilute the strong effect of his name.

BEST-IN-CLASS MARKETING

Once a buyer sees that a firm has a transferrable brand, they will want to see a working marketing plan, so be sure you're ready. To evaluate an existing marketing plan, it's important to assess its components and determine if it aligns with the firm's mission, vision, and values. Then, a good marketing plan should have a detailed list of actions and campaigns aimed at growing the business. Specifically, this involves identifying the target audience and creating a strong brand message that speaks to this audience's needs and desires. A content marketing strategy that resonates with the audience is crucial because it positions the firm as a thought leader in its space.

A successful marketing plan also requires a comprehensive understanding of the channels that will be used to reach the target audience, such as social media, email marketing, and/or paid advertising. The plan should have well-defined expected returns and outcomes, which can help determine the budget for each component. Circuit breakers should be in place for all expenditures to ensure the budget stays within acceptable limits.

To maximize effectiveness, a good marketing plan should diversify among marketing sources, including different channels and methods. This helps reach a wider audience and increases brand exposure. Additionally, the plan should leave room to test campaigns before significant financial resources are allocated to them, which minimizes risk and allows for necessary adjustments to be made before a full launch.

And that brings up an important point. Data is key to ensuring that a marketing plan is working. A well-run marketing department or team tracks a number of data points in order to evaluate the success or failure of their marketing plan. At a minimum, the firm should be tracking:

- Performance for each individual campaign
- Website metrics
- Return on investment
  - Each campaign
  - Client acquisition cost
  - Lifetime client value

Knowing these numbers quantifies the marketing plan, which allows the marketing team to make quick decisions. The performance of each campaign is defined in advance because a limit is set on numbers (such as the client acquisition cost), a goal is set for the lifetime client value, and expectations are delineated for website numbers. Everything a buyer likes to know.

In addition, the buyer will want to see that there is a feedback loop built into the marketing plan. Are you using the data to make ongoing adjustments to the plan? Does the plan have enough room in it to allow for changes as you go?

In marketing, it's important to test out new campaigns before committing significant resources to them. Jim Collins' theory of firing bullets and then cannonballs is a great way to approach this.[5] Essentially, it means testing small, low-cost marketing efforts (the bullets) before investing heavily in a particular strategy (the cannonballs). This allows you to gain valuable insights into what works and what doesn't before making a big investment. It's a great way to minimize risk and ensure that your marketing efforts are aligned with your overall mission and goals. By taking the time to test out different ideas and strategies, you can improve the effectiveness of your marketing plan and ensure that you're getting the most out of your resources.

Sebastian realized fairly early on that his marketing team didn't have the ability to execute, much less create, a solid marketing plan. When we showed him the return on investment for their efforts, the team's response was, "We don't know how to fix it." He took decisive action and turned over the entire marketing team so he would be able to see the results that a best-in-class marketing department could produce. It was a hard decision to make, but Sebastian realized the team he had couldn't get him to the next level. This is an example of his willingness to make tough decisions and execute them — even when they didn't feel good — for the overall benefit

---

5 Jim Collins, *Good to Great: Why Some Companies Make the Leap... and Others Don't.* New York, New York: Harper Business, 2001.

of the firm. And that is why his firm grew from $5.5 million to $24 million in seven years.

SUMMARY

Evaluating your brand and marketing plan is critical to the successful sale of your law firm. Ask yourself if your brand is transferrable and if you're running a best-in-class marketing plan with a data-driven analysis component. If not, it's time to take action. Start by identifying gaps in your current plan and then determine what steps need to be taken to improve. This may involve a brand refresh, a realignment of your mission, vision, and values, and/or a more diversified approach to your marketing sources. Remember the importance of firing bullets before cannonballs, testing and tracking your campaigns, and setting circuit breakers on all expenditures. By taking a deliberate and strategic approach to your marketing strategy, you can position your firm for long-term growth and success.

CHAPTER 12

SALES AND INTAKE

THE SALES AND intake process is particularly interesting from a valuation standpoint. Law firms have historically had their lawyers doing sales — without any sales training. While buyers may not be surprised by this, they are pleasantly surprised when a business has developed a strong sales and intake process, and they're willing to pay more for it. The key to an efficient sales and intake process lies in the understanding that it involves both sales and psychology.

Buyers are looking for a business that can build a solid relationship with potential clients. Specifically, they want a firm that displays the ability to quickly establish a rapport with clients and one that provides responsive service to deliver the results that clients expect. This winning combination of sales acumen and emotional intelligence demonstrates that the business is well-equipped to generate higher conversion rates and achieve higher client satisfaction rates. For teams to reach these goals, it's essential to have the right team composition, effective technology, and well-designed systems in place.

TEAM COMPOSITION

When a potential buyer evaluates your business, they will be particularly interested in the design of your intake team. For a larger firm, an organized, dedicated intake team of at least three people demonstrates your commitment to client onboarding and customer satisfaction. A well-structured team should be responsible for taking new calls, following up on leads, and maintaining relationships with existing clients (ensuring that their needs are met and they are happy with your services).

If your practice area demands after-hours call handling, showcase this capability. It will appeal to potential buyers and indicates your readiness to accommodate clients who cannot contact you during regular business hours, which gives your business a competitive edge. Additionally, if your client base includes non-English speakers, having team members who are fluent in other languages displays your commitment to providing excellent service to a diverse clientele.

Potential buyers will also appreciate your attention to detail when it comes to job titles. Rather than simply referring to your intake team as "intake specialists," use titles like "consultation coordinator" or "client care team member," which sends a message of professionalism and empathy.

By carefully considering and presenting the composition and roles of your intake team, you demonstrate to potential buyers that your business is well-organized, client-focused, and worth their investment.

TECHNOLOGY

As a buyer, it's crucial to evaluate the technology being used by the business in its sales and intake process. It's important to see how a company utilizes an intake system with seamless integration across all sources and software. This ensures efficient data collection and management, which ultimately contributes to the smooth running of the firm.

Potential buyers pay particular attention to whether a business has automated follow-up systems in place. These include email campaigns that stay in touch with potential clients who didn't convert, as well as post-call follow-up campaigns for potential clients who didn't sign up initially. These systems demonstrate that the company is proactive when it comes to maintaining relationships with potential clients. This is important because, over time, proactive systems can lead to increased conversion rates.

Buyers will also consider whether the company offers the convenience of electronic signatures for fee agreements, text communication with prospects, and website chat features. These capabilities make it easier for clients to engage with the firm and help the company stay competitive in today's digital landscape. Additionally, they'll evaluate whether a firm utilizes call tracking and monitors conversion metrics, as this data-driven approach can optimize the intake process and contribute to the business's overall success.

Systems: Training

Once you have the composition of your team, it's important to make sure they are trained and equipped to handle your potential clients when they contact the firm. As with any other position in the firm, training is vitally important to the success of your intake team.

The training course should include three main topics:

- Software training
- Sales training
- Empathy training

At a minimum, you should have a software training manual or a list of online training courses that are required for all salespeople. As firms become more technologically advanced and rely more on software that is integrated throughout the firm, it is vitally important that the intake team understands precisely how to use their software, especially since the information it generates populates other parts of the system. Being confident and quick smooths the path not only for the legal and billing teams but also for the clients.

A buyer is going to want to see that you have hired true salespeople and have not simply promoted the receptionist (or worse, are just having them do both jobs). Selling requires both a precise set of skills and a specific personality. I say hire for the personality and train for the skills. Sales training is probably not something to do in-house.

Spending money to train your salespeople and giving them the opportunity to take refresher courses always creates a good ROI (return on investment).

The last piece of training is empathy training. Potential clients aren't usually excited about coming to an attorney. Generally, they have lived with and worried about some problem until they can no longer stand it. That is when they pick up the phone or grab their computer to contact the firm. Having a team that understands that and shows empathy for the person on the other end of the line is vital for building the rapport that makes the difference between a client and a lost opportunity.

Please also be aware that intake teams sometimes develop tough skin because of what they hear on the phone all day. Imagine how hard it is to hear about horrible life-changing accidents if you work for a personal injury firm, the dire straits a potential client may be in if they need to file for bankruptcy, or the physical and/or emotional abuse a spouse calling about a divorce may be enduring. In order to connect with that potential client, your intake team needs to listen and empathize in order to understand their situation. This can take a toll. Because of this, your empathy training needs to have a component where the team members get occasional mental health checks — especially if you have a practice area with high conflict or that deals with emotional and/or physical trauma.

Systems: Feedback

The last part of a strong sales or intake team is the feedback loop. You need to know what's working and what isn't. All the information collected through data (such as call tracking and conversion rates) is essential for the marketing group so they can make sure they are putting money where it is most effective. Recording and listening to calls is not only helpful for a salesperson who is being trained or having a hard time; it is also a great way to recognize somebody's accomplishments and illustrate to the team how to best handle particular situations.

John Boyd, a fighter pilot and military strategist, developed a decision process that defined how to react to an event. He called this the OODA loop — Observe, Orient, Decide, Act. He took this concept a step further with the creation of Boyd's Law, which states that the speed of iteration beats the quality of iteration.[6] Simply put, how quickly you can change is better than how perfectly you can change. Feedback loops allow the firm to make changes — to iterate. The ability to quickly learn and adjust is incredibly attractive to a buyer.

SUMMARY

A dedicated and diverse intake team with a strong focus on client care lays the foundation for an effective sales process. State-of-the-art technology enables seamless communication, data tracking, and efficiency, while a comprehensive training program ensures the team is prepared to excel in their roles. Last of all, a well-established

---

6 Business901, "Boyd's Law of Iteration: Speed Beats…," February 12, 2010, https://business901.com/blog1/boyds-law-of-iteration-speed-beats-quality/.

feedback loop fosters continuous improvement and enhances the overall client experience. With these key components in place, a buyer can be confident in a law firm's value and future growth potential.

CHAPTER 13

OPERATIONS

EVERY LAW FIRM operates differently, so if you thought this chapter was going to be a how-to manual for managing a law firm, I'm sorry to disappoint you. But what I can tell you is that all well-run and, therefore, valuable firms have two things in common: clear descriptions of roles and responsibilities and well-documented processes. Potential buyers want to know that the back-end operations are well run and that they won't require a lot of set up or time from the new owner.

ROLES AND RESPONSIBILITIES

When you started your firm, it was probably just you — maybe with a paralegal. You did everything. You were the owner, attorney, bookkeeper, office manager, paralegal, receptionist, file clerk, and chief bottle washer. No documentation needed. But as the firm grew, you were able to hire people and offload responsibilities.

Notice that I said offload and not delegate. In the early stages of growth, owners are more likely to simply dump, or offload, tasks onto people. You might think you have delegated, but that usually implies parameters, oversight, and structure. Parameters, oversight, and structure are rarely found in small firms. These things arrive later when the firm is more developed and you finally implement an organizational chart.

Actually, an org chart doesn't go far enough. A better term is what EOS® founder Gino Wickman calls The Accountability Chart®. While traditional org charts show roles and reporting structures, The Accountability Chart® takes it further and shows responsibilities. It answers questions like: What are the five to seven major job functions for each role? What does this role have to do? What has been delegated to this role?

An accountability chart increases focus, discipline, and accountability. It allows everyone to understand not only their role within the business but also the role of others and how everyone fits into the firm as a whole. They see how their work impacts the work of others, which helps create cohesiveness and accountability to their teammates (and not just to their boss).

It also allows the firm to quickly assess what Jim Collins calls the "right person, right seat" mindset.[7] With this approach, leaders ask questions to determine whether an individual is a good fit for the business: Are they the right person for the firm? Are they a core value match?

---

7   Collins, *Good to Great.*

(We'll talk about this more in the next chapter when we talk about culture.)

If they are the right person, then as the employer, you'll need to attack the next part: Are they in the right seat? Do they understand the job and its requirements? Are the five to seven major job functions for their job spelled out on the accountability chart? If so, does this person have the skill set to do that job? If yes, great. If not, do they have the capability to learn, and do you have the time and bandwidth to teach them? Having the right person in the right seat makes all the difference.

PROCESS

While an accountability chart details each employee's responsibilities, you want them to own their responsibilities. At the same time, as their employer, you also need to hold them accountable. And you want the team (their peers) to hold them accountable as well. Once they understand where they stand in the company and what the work is, it's important to give them a roadmap of how that work gets done, and you do that by creating processes.

Let's go back to when you started the firm. As chief of everything, you knew how to do everything. And even as you hired people, you were the one with all the answers. You knew where every document was stored, you knew how things had been done in the past, and you could answer every question. The people you hired in the early days also likely have an immense amount of information locked in their brains. We call that institutional knowledge.

And while institutional knowledge is valuable to those who hold it, it is even more valuable when it is out of heads and accessible to everybody. Now, I am not judging the people with the information. In fact, at my company, I am one of them. But I am amazed when somebody struggles with something or spends time reinventing something that I have already done, and it all happens because nobody asked whether we had done it before. In my defense, it didn't occur to me to tell anybody about it any earlier. And there, you can see the inefficiency of institutional knowledge.

Sebastian tackled the systematization of his firm early — earlier than any firm I have ever seen, and I attribute that to his brother, Larry, who was the COO at the time. Larry had come from a large organization and was a systems-driven kinda' guy. Sebastian walked into his office one day to see all kinds of processes mapped out on the walls. At the time, Sebastian thought Larry had gone a little overboard, but now he is grateful.

What Larry did was talk to each person who held a role (for example, all the paralegals). He then figured out what part of the job each of them did that was exceptional. He took that information back to his office and engineered a process for each role that was, frankly, genius. When he implemented the new processes, Sebastian's firm experienced better speed, quality, efficiency, and accountability. A byproduct was the ability to cross-train people so that nobody became such a key employee that they couldn't go on vacation. And boy, was it easier to onboard new employees. Because Larry did the work of documenting, he established how the firm made decisions about everything.

Did Larry go into a little too much detail? Probably. His processes are pretty intricate and probably better suited to a manufacturing company. Do yours need to be this detailed? Absolutely not. When we talk about documenting processes, a buyer is looking for the top 20 percent to be documented. Find the 20 percent of your processes that cover 80 percent of the work, and hopefully, include what makes you special or stand out from your competitors.

DON'T OVER-OPERATIONALIZE

Documentation does not mean what I used to think — looooooooong procedures with pictures and circles with arrows pointing to the enter button saying, "CLICK HERE." You just need to give them the roadmap. Again, let's go back to the 80/20 Rule. Find the 20 percent of the steps — the major steps — that produce 80 percent of the results. That's what needs to be documented — not every little thing. Once you have identified those major steps, briefly explain the who, what, where, when, and how to get each done.

I reflected on this 80/20 split one Sunday afternoon as a plane I was on headed toward DFW. When we were about twenty feet off the runway, the pilot aborted the landing. He jerked the plane up, and I was slammed into my seat. As we quickly gained altitude, I heard the landing gear retract. Or did it come down? I wasn't sure. But what I did know is how a pilot's procedures are written. Do their checklists have every single little thing on them? You may be surprised to discover that they don't. Why? Because they want pilots to be able to make decisions. And they found that if a pilot has a detailed checklist, they will go down the checklist and not think. Two things can happen when they don't think. Items get forgotten or skipped, and they don't use their judgment. I'm glad they left room for judgment because as we were landing that Sunday, my pilot looked down the runway and saw another plane in our way. That's why he aborted the touchdown.

Isadore Sharp, founder of the Four Seasons Hotels and Resorts, says it's important to "systematize the predictable so you can humanize the exceptional."[8] Your teams are dealing with humans in some of the most stressful situations of their lives — divorce, immigration, litigation, prosecution, death. None of these are fun for your clients. Be sure to leave room for your employees to be human — this will set you apart from the other firms.

SUMMARY

A buyer wants to see a well-run business that they won't need to micromanage. When you have employees who understand their place in the firm, own their responsibilities, are accountable to their boss, teammates, and themselves, and have documented procedures on how to deliver those responsibilities, the owner does not have to be involved in the day-to-day operations of the firm. When looking at a firm from a valuation standpoint, nothing makes it more attractive than one that puts few (or no) demands on the owner.

---

8   Paton and Gonzalez, *Process!*, 16.

CHAPTER 14

PEOPLE

YOUR TEAM IS the lifeblood of your firm. Without them, your firm will have very little value. If you can get this component dialed in, it can vastly increase your multiple. I believe there are two parts to dialing in the people side of your business — culture and human resources. You have to win at both of them. But let's start with culture because if you can't get that right, nothing else will matter.

CULTURE

Culture is the way people feel at your firm. It is the way you treat them; it's the environment. It is what will drive the cohesiveness of (or the wedge between) your team. And culture starts with your core values.

In most companies, core values are a few inspirational words on posters slapped up on the walls in hallways, conference rooms, or break rooms. Or they are a page or two given to new hires and never addressed again after day one. They have little meaning and virtually nothing to do with the company. In fact, in most cases, you could swap out the core values from one firm to another, and no one would know the difference. You know the type: integrity, teamwork, loyalty, humility, compassion. And there's my personal favorite: values. Really? Your core value is that you have core values? These are nothing more than marketing run amok.

True core values explain to the team who you are as a group, what you believe in, and how you behave. They are used to hire, fire, promote, and reward employees. They are part of everyday conversations and are definitely part of quarterly and annual reviews. They are a living, breathing part of your business — because they define who you are as a firm.

> **True core values explain to the team who you are as a group, what you believe in, and how you behave.**

But how do you implement core values? This was a place where Sebastian struggled. He believed he had a strong company culture. The firm focuses on clients who are military veterans, and virtually everyone in the firm has either served in the military or is the child or spouse of someone who served. There was a clear culture of command and control that allowed people to delegate tasks and be certain that they would be completed — and completed on time.

However, Sebastian came to realize that wasn't a company culture. It was a reporting structure. The culture he believed he had only permeated the leadership team. The rest of the firm didn't feel it. He didn't understand how intentional he needed to be about finding moments to rally the team.

Sebastian hired a consultant at $20K a week to help push the culture through the entire firm. Previously, his people thought they were "fighting" for their clients and had that combative mindset in all their interactions — even with each other. He realized that didn't build a great team. They shifted to an "in-it-to-win-it" mentality, and he watched his people come together as a squad. Now, his team is celebrating wins, and most importantly, individuals are empowered to take on their own missions for the greater good of the firm.

Most people associate culture with their boss, and there is an immense amount of research on the costs of a bad boss. In an article for *Inc. Magazine*, Maeghan Ouimet said that 65 percent of employees would take a new boss over a pay raise.[9] She went on to say that it's not what bosses do that makes them bad; it's what they don't do. The top five misses are:

1. Fails to inspire
2. Accepts mediocrity
3. Lacks clear vision and direction
4. Unable to collaborate and be a team player
5. Fails to walk the talk

---

9   Ouimet, Maeghan. "The Real Cost of Bad Bosses." *Inc. Magazine*, November 15, 2012. https://www.inc.com/maeghan-ouimet/real-cost-bad-bosses.html.

When I look at these misses, I see a failure of core values. If our leaders understand and live the core values of the firm and hire people who share those same core values, they can't help but inspire. They won't tolerate anything but the best, and the direction will be crystal clear to everybody.

Core values bind the team together, bosses included. And frankly, if a leader isn't walking the talk, if they aren't a core value match, they shouldn't be part of the firm. They are doing more damage than good by being there. No matter how talented or smart they are, if they aren't a match, they need to go — even if they are an amazing rainmaker. That is how you create team members who will walk through fire for each other. And that is an attractive team to purchase and a team a buyer is willing to pay more for.

THE IMPORTANCE OF HR

How do you get that team? That's the second part of the people side of the business — the often unsexy, mechanical part — human resources. HR is very process-oriented, so you need to make sure you not only have the processes dialed in but also that they are aligned with your core values.

For example, let's say one of your core values is "team first." Sounds great. But if you are paying significantly below market value so you can pass those savings along to your client, that's definitely not putting the team first. That sounds like "client first" — and your team will feel it. A best-in-class HR team creates processes and makes sure they align with the firm's core values.

So, what are these all-important HR processes?

- Hiring
- Onboarding
- Training
- Career Development

Hiring

The first step is the hiring process. How does your firm find the right people? Jim Collins is famous for talking about having the right people in the right seats.[10] The right people, in this sense, are a core value match for your firm.

Before you get serious about any potential candidate, you need to make sure they are a core value match. Southwest Airlines was famous for doing this. I was lucky enough to attend a workshop with Colleen Barrett, who built their remarkable culture. She emphasized that asking questions relating to core values in the very first interview was key to finding the right people.

Once you know you have the right person, you can move to Collins' "right seat" part of the equation and start interviewing for skill set. This usually involves a skills test of some kind related to the work this person will be doing.

Then, in addition to interviewing with their potential supervisor, the candidate should meet with a peer and probably you, as the founder of the firm. Each of you should fill out a feedback form, and each interviewer (including the person doing the skill set interview) should assess the person based on how they perceive the candidate

---

10 Collins, *Good to Great*.

will fit with the firm's core values. These evaluation forms should be compiled and given to the person who is ultimately responsible for making the hiring decision so it can be an informed one.

Onboarding

Once they are hired, you need to onboard and train new employees. I'm going to repeat that tired saying, "You never get a second chance to make a first impression." Annoying but true. And it really holds with your new hires. They are excited about coming on board, but you have not built any trust with them yet. The interview process was nothing but a series of promises. Now is the time to deliver on those.

Are all those annoying forms they need to fill out easily accessible and ready for them on the first day? Is their computer set up and ready to go? Nothing is worse for a new hire than walking into an office and feeling like the firm forgot they were starting. It makes them feel like you don't care. And I can't imagine that's congruent with your core values. Do you have a timeline with a list of to-dos to make sure this doesn't happen? Having that in place is gold for a buyer.

Training

I already talked about the importance of processes and how they improve the speed, quality, and efficiency of a firm. Your training program needs to address a few different things.

- Core Values
- Companywide information
- Job-specific tasks

First, it should teach the core values and culture of the firm. It needs to help acclimate new hires to the technology and systems used and introduce them to companywide procedures and standards.

Once you have addressed this basic level of training, the program should become job specific. What does a paralegal need to know versus an attorney versus somebody in intake? Explain their individual roles and responsibilities. Show them the scripts, the forms, and the measurables by which they will be held accountable. A best-in-class training program uses different types of learning — video, reading, and auditory — because each person learns in a different manner. And then, testing needs to be completed to ensure the new hire is competent in all the necessary skills. Be sure to go over the retention of the information, and check the fit of a new hire in thirty-, sixty-, and ninety-day reviews.

Having training automated alleviates a big headache for a potential buyer. If automating isn't feasible, the next best thing is to have it in a format that any employee can access and use to train any new hire to do any job. If a buyer wants to scale the firm, that option is on the table if a documented employee training program is already in place. They'll know exactly how long it will take to get a new employee up to speed and productive in the firm. They can also see by looking at the training program what that level of competence will be.

Career Development

Your responsibility to your employees and training doesn't end with their ninety-day review. Sebastian was great at hiring people. He was also great at what he called "the red wedding" (firing people). After a while, his team stabilized some, but we noticed there was a problem. He had a great leadership team, and he had great people doing the work, but as he was rocketing through to $15 million, he didn't have any middle managers. And the firm wasn't doing anything to develop them.

Your employees want a career path. How can they stay with your firm, continue to grow, get more responsibility, and not end up doing the same boring, repetitive job for years on end? And from your side, when people retire or leave, who is sitting on the bench, ready to step up to the plate to be your next set of leaders?

Developing career paths and leaders is a partnership between the firm and motivated employees. As the owner, you need to be willing to invest in these people and get them the training they need (which will probably come from outside the firm and will definitely cost money). And you probably won't see an immediate return. The employee needs to be motivated enough to look at the firm, see options, have ambition, be willing to put in extra effort to learn new skills, and do the uncomfortable — all for a payoff that might not come for a couple of years. It is a risk on both sides, but one your firm can't afford not to take. By investing in your future, you are ensuring the continued success of the firm — and that translates into more value when selling. It is one less thing a buyer has to do themselves. It means there will be less work on their part after the acquisition. Any effort you can save the buyer equals more money in your pocket at the time of sale.

SUMMARY

People are your most important resource, and turnover is expensive. It is much cheaper to hire right the first time, train them, and retain them until, well, forever. Binding employees to the firm by creating a true team that will do the hard thing, sacrifice for others, and pull in the same direction keeps employees from leaving. And all of that starts with uncovering your core values and making them an everyday part of the discussion in your firm.

CHAPTER 15

PRODUCTION

TRULY UNDERSTANDING THE metrics that drive a firm is one of the keys to the kingdom if the kingdom you are seeking is a profitable firm. Law firms make money by moving work through their firm. The faster you can do this, with the least amount of friction, the better.

Many owners spend years playing whack-a-mole. As each new constriction point pops up, they identify it, solve the problem, and then wait for the next constraint to appear. If you have done this — great. If you haven't, this chapter will help you identify key places to look for problems and then explain how to fix them. Because the faster, better, and smoother the work flows through your firm, the higher the valuation.

Streamlining production processes involves four specific areas:

- Understanding capacity
- Setting and tracking billing goals

- Holding your team accountable
- Creating efficient working groups

CAPACITY AND BILLING

When firms first contact us, they are almost always spending too much on payroll, and that is the result of one of three things:

- They are paying their employees too much in relation to what they are producing and collecting.
- They aren't charging enough for their services.
- They have hired too much capacity.

Compensation

We run firms based on the rule of thirds — one-third of revenue goes to payroll, one-third goes to overhead, and one-third goes to profit. If we adhere to this, each employee must bill and collect 3X their cost of employment. As with most things, it's not actually that simple. Not all employees do billable or client-facing work. Your bookkeeper, office manager, and receptionist don't do any legal work. And if you are a smaller firm, you probably have team members whose jobs are part billable and part nonbillable. For this reason, we want the younger people on the team to be closer to a 5X return.

This was one of the hardest nuts for us to crack with Sebastian. It took a couple of years and a number of compensation structures to finally get it right. First, he had been giving all of his attorneys one-third of what they billed, whether it was collected or not. Sebastian was paying commission on revenue regardless of whether he had received it or not. We lowered the amount the attorneys received from one-third to closer to one-fourth and changed it to apply only to collected dollars, not the amount billed. Since most attorneys don't like it when you get rid of their cushy pay plan, we created a bonus structure where they could actually make more money if they brought in cases and worked more than the bare minimum. It was a win-win situation.

Billing Rates

Getting a 3X or 5X return on your billable employees assumes, in an hourly or flat-fee firm, that you have set their hourly billing rates and goals at an appropriate level.

If you thought, "Yikes, I don't have billing goals," we have identified an easy fix. Everybody gets a billing goal. And before you dismiss this because you bill a flat fee or have contingency agreements so you don't track time, I will tell you that every firm has at least one metric that is predictive of revenue.

For one firm we worked with, it was sending out settlement packages. We knew that when they sent out a settlement package, they would get an offer and then get a check within a certain amount of time (on average). Their billing goal was the number of settlement packages. What is the one metric that is predictive of your revenue? That should be your goal.

And if you are an hourly firm, your billable rates are part art and part science. When you hire somebody, look at the going salaries in your area, multiply by 3X to 5X, decide how much the culture of your firm dictates they work (billing goal), and divide that out to find their hourly rate. If it is too high, you either need to pay them less or make them work more. If the hourly rate looks pretty low, you might want to pay them more so they feel valued, re-evaluate their billing goal, or adjust the rate to what you think it should be and know that you have room to give them raises in the future.

Capacity

People are the thing firms most often overspend on, and therefore, they are the thing that most often devalues a firm. If you can get compensation and billing goals balanced, the next place to look to improve value is the firm's capacity.

Too many times, we have seen firms with significantly more staff than they need to produce the revenue they are generating. I had a sales call once with a firm in Florida. I am notorious for doing quick math on calls, and after a few questions, I told him he had enough people on his team to be doing $2.7 million in revenue. He responded that he was only doing $1.2 million. No wonder he was losing money every month!

To calculate your capacity, simply multiply the billing goals by the billing rates or average matter value. That will tell you how much work you can move through your firm.

If your revenue is lower than your capacity, then people aren't producing. You need to find out why. If they don't have the cases, go talk to marketing. If they don't know how to work the cases, go talk to HR about the training process or to operations about the procedures.

But if they have the work, know how to do it, and it's not getting done, it's likely one of two problems. Either they aren't being held accountable, or there is a bottleneck in the system, and they have to wait to do their part of the work.

ACCOUNTABILITY

Accountability is hard because it never ends. It is a week-in, week-out discussion with each billable person. Everybody should have a goal, and each employee should get a report once a week that says whether or not they are on track. They should also have a discussion with their supervisor about why they did or did not hit their goal, what worked or didn't work, and what they are committing to do differently next week. While not a glamorous discussion, it is one of the most worthwhile things that can happen in a law firm because this is how you create a culture of accountability. And for those people who don't make their goals? I learned a phrase a long time ago that I love, "Manage them up or manage them out."

Holding employees accountable was a problem Sebastian had to overcome. He had billing goals for each of them, but he wasn't holding them accountable, and there were no consequences if an attorney missed their goals. Repeatedly. For months on end. He had to start "managing them out," and as hard as it was, he noticed that the morale picked up among the rest of his team. And so did the amount of work moving through his firm.

DEFINING A TEAM

If your production team has the work, knows how to do it, is being held accountable, and the work's still not getting done, you need to look to the next problem — defining the team. The solution for this one is the same as the solution for understanding how many people you need to hire in general. Calculating the overall capacity of the firm is great, but having attorney capacity that is equal to paralegal capacity is almost always wrong. Why? Because it is rare that a case requires equal time from each type of employee.

Most attorneys know this instinctively and hire (mostly) appropriately. A really valuable law firm has done the studies and the math to have this down to a science. They understand, by case type, the ratio of each type of support staff to one attorney. They can define their team.

Defining a team in hourly billed law firms is easy. Take the last ten to fifteen cases that were closed, add up all the hours spent (by employee type), divide by the number of cases, and then divide by the total attorney time. This will show you how many non-lawyer employees are needed for every one attorney. Do this for every type of case, and you can start to build a custom team.

In flat fee and contingency practices, it is a little harder. Of course, my preference is that you record your time for a few months, and we extrapolate from there, but that isn't going to happen. I've quit fighting that fight. The alternative is to sit down, usually with all the people who work on a case, and go through the case step by step and estimate how much time it takes. You will probably underestimate, so I would add 20 percent to compensate for this. But at least you have an approximation.

Once you've done the math, you can see that for every attorney, you need 1.5 paralegals and .5 legal assistants. I totally made up these numbers, but go with me here — I'm going to make up a few more numbers.

The attorneys have a billing goal of 173 settlement packages a year. The average matter lasts nine months, with an average matter value of $5,764. On average, it takes 8.3 hours of attorney time.

This team of two full-time people and two part-time people will produce almost $1,000,000 in a year if they are held accountable. Marketing tells us they expect to bring in about twenty cases per week. 20 X 52 = 1,040 total new cases. If we divide that by the attorney billing goal of 173, we need six teams. That means six attorneys, nine paralegals, and three legal assistants. We have the *perfect* amount of capacity. We are not overspending on our people at all. Why? Because we defined our team.

Once the team is defined, it is easy to scale that team. Who will max out first on capacity? It is rare that numbers are quite as round as my example. Usually, you see that one person is .8 and another is 1.1. That person carrying 1.1 is going to max out faster, so if you are growing, you need to hire another one of them first.

The Pod System

Now that you have defined the team, have you thought about creating a working group with them? So often, firms distribute work in a haphazard way. An attorney walks out of their office and grabs the paralegal who is available at that moment to help with something. Everybody on the team is constantly switching from working with this person to working with that person — and each person has a different work style, a different way of prepping documents, and a different way of wanting documents prepared.

In the "old days," each attorney had their own paralegal — and this had a lot of merit. Studies have shown there is a high productivity cost when switching staff members. By creating a working group — we call them pods — the team gets used to working with each other. They develop a shorthand that creates efficiencies. Instruction time is reduced because pod-mates can anticipate what is coming next and how it needs to be done. Anything that reduces friction in moving work through your firm increases its value.

This was the problem Sebastian overcame when it came to moving work through his firm. He saw the merits and efficiencies of working in pods and also saw how he could compensate the pods based on pod profit. By looking at the bottom line and running each pod like a mini law firm, he was able to align the employees' compensation and focus with his own.

SUMMARY

Streamlining your law firm's production comes down to understanding capacity, setting and tracking billing goals, holding your team accountable, and creating efficient working groups. When a buyer looks at a firm that has these things in place, they know they can easily scale the practice without overspending on capacity. That's valuable.

CHAPTER 16

TECHNOLOGY

I WAS AWARDED a designation called the Chartered Financial Analyst®. Basically, it's like taking three successively harder bar exams once a year, three years in a row (if law school only covered the material for first level, and you didn't get your designation until you passed all three levels). Can you tell I still have a little PTSD from that experience? Anyway, let's go back to that story about me consistently failing one section of the test and the family friend who owned the review course telling me to walk away from the section.

I hate to tell you to walk away from any section of your law firm, but if you have limited time and resources and you have to walk away from something, it is technology. The legal industry has never been an early adopter of technology. You basically practice law the same way they did 500 years ago. There are a few things that have changed: the typewriter, word processing, and online research (which was a complete game-changer). But otherwise, it's essentially the same.

I was recently talking to Ashton, one of our new clients. He has hired data entry people because he bought a firm, and all their records are on paper. They are literally manually inputting information into Ashton's practice management system.

Is that what buyers want? Certainly not. However, when your firm is being acquired, even if both firms have technology, chances are slim they will be the same programs. A large tech project is often an expected part of the transaction, and buyers are prepared for this considerable expense.

What does this mean to the bottom-line value of your firm? Don't invest a bunch of time and money in implementing something that a prospective buyer might not even want.

That being said, a well-run, profitable firm uses technology in as many places as possible. And that technology is integrated to create data that flows freely, creates a holistic picture of what is happening in the firm, and drives decision-making. That kind of technology increases the value of the firm. Why? Because you can give a buyer data that backs up your claims, and you can demonstrate the operations of your firm.

Buyers want to see technology investments in three main places: financials, operations, and marketing.

FINANCIALS

I am starting with financials because accounting software is probably the first piece of software that an owner invests in. And I will also put a caveat here to what I said earlier — if you don't keep your books electronically, a buyer will care. That is a big deal. They will want to see how you run your firm, and flipping through ledgers will not make them happy. If you hand over spreadsheets you designed yourself, it's going to be even worse.

There are all kinds of accounting programs out there. At Cathcap, QuickBooks Online is our personal preference. Is QuickBooks Online perfect? No. But it gets the job done, offering a very user-friendly experience at a relatively inexpensive cost.

But there are other options. Do your research and understand from the outset how easy it is to get your data out of the system. Someday, you might outgrow it and want to migrate to a practice management system with integrated financials, and if all your current system can do is print out financial statements, you lose all the transactional detail. And the bar association cares about that transactional detail in your Trust or IOLTA accounts. Additionally, many states conduct random audits that can go back a number of years and require you to be able to prove transaction-level detail. This is one of the reasons we caution against using some of the easy-to-operate software. It lacks the back-end functionality that becomes so important later on.

There are a number of practice management systems (PMS) that have the accounting function built in. Historically, these have been little more than a bolted widget that did some simple math and kept a log. However, in recent years, they have improved dramatically. If your firm has a PMS, by all means, use it. You will be able to see some information about things like collections and billing that would otherwise be harder to obtain.

PRACTICE MANAGEMENT SYSTEMS

And since we are talking about PMS, these are probably the second piece of software law firms get. I think of them as electronic filing cabinets and Rolodexes that do a lot of other things, like help draft documents, perform automatic calendaring, conduct conflict checks, keep your time, and do the billing! Can all of this be done on paper? Absolutely. But it can also be done faster and more accurately by a computer. Not to mention that if you have software that is cloud-based, it allows your team to access any file at any time, from any place. No more wandering down the hall asking people if they have the Jones file.

The organizational aspect of a PMS is great. But its true benefit to the bottom line of your firm's value is its ability to give you actionable data. Your PMS can tell you which cases are the most profitable, which clients pay the fastest, which employee is the most productive, and how to price your services more accurately. This type of information allows you to create a profitable firm. And a profitable firm is worth more.

MARKETING

In many ways, marketing is a numbers game. How many people know about you, how many people contacted you, how many of those are qualified, how many booked sales calls, and how many signed? Once you know those numbers, it is a simple matter of tweaking or driving specific ones to get the results you want. The challenge is knowing the numbers.

And that is where technology comes in. The larger a firm, the more leads that come in, and the more necessary some kind of Client Relationship Management system (CRM) becomes. A CRM tracks potential clients, "drips" information on them to convince them to become clients, and chronicles a potential client's journey through the sales process. This is where you find all that juicy data that helps you increase your conversion rates.

Again, the bigger the firm, the more potential clients and marketing channels you'll have. This is when technology really becomes valuable because it can be used to track everything. At some point, you can add call-tracking software that captures the phone number a potential client called, so it knows if they came in from an ad, a billboard, or a particular website. Your marketing firm or marketing team is tracking all the web traffic to understand exactly where clients are coming from on the internet.

INTEGRATION

The key to all the software, not just marketing software, is that it needs to be integrated. And to integrate it, you need to think about a client's journey from prospect to client to satisfied former client. When I say the software needs to be integrated, I mean that it not only needs to be connected to the other software, but you need to ensure the language and terms are consistent throughout every piece. If you call it Divorce with Kids in the CRM, then it must be called Divorce with Kids in your PMS and everywhere else. It can't be Divorce with Children in your accounting software. You need to make sure you are tracking expenditures in the accounting software by the same name you are using in your CRM system so you can understand what the return on investment was for a particular campaign or marketing activity.

When things are consistent, information can be pulled from any system and used in combination with information from any other system to give you, or your buyer, insights into how the firm works and the ability to make fast decisions with few regrets.

Once we had implemented and integrated technology, Sebastian had his new marketing team tracking all their information, his attorneys were being held accountable for their billing goals, and he started to get real-time data about his firm. For the first time, he could get a bird's eye view of how everything worked, helping him make better decisions. And remember, it is Sebastian's ability to make quick decisions and execute them that helped him have such incredible growth over the seven years I've known him.

SUMMARY

Technology really is a conundrum for law firms. Because the industry has been slow to adopt, buyers have come to expect that any purchase will probably include a big technology implementation project, which is a headache. So, if you don't have the tech, don't sweat it because that is what most buyers expect.

However, if you do have it, you are alleviating a big pain point. It gives you the data to demonstrate the value of the firm, and you'll be able to sell it for a higher price.

As with many things in this book, it comes down to time and money. Do you have the money to do a software revamp or implementation? Secondly, if you are doing an implementation, will you have enough time to gather demonstrative data to aid in your sale? If not, it won't be worth the time and effort.

SEBASTIAN'S CASE STUDY

While Sebastian intended to keep his firm, the actions he took to improve operations and profitability were the same as if he had wanted to sell. He focused on the big items first, becoming more profitable by rightsizing his payroll and documenting processes.

His reorganization of the firm's reporting structure gave clarity to his team, and his focus on culture created a mentality where every employee was "in it to win it" together. Because Sebastian had a long timeframe, he was able to systematically attack problems and overhaul his firm. This process continues today as he finds additional tweaks that advance both top and bottom-line growth.

	Beginning of Engagement	End of Engagement
Revenue	$5.5MM	$18.3MM
Net Income	.006MM = 1%	2.3MM = 12%
SDE	.7MM = 12%	3.0MM = 17%
Price		
Est. Multiple of SDE	2.5	4.0
Estimated Price	$1.7MM	$12.1MM
Timeframe	4 years	
Type of Buyer	Family Succession	

What Sebastian Did to Improve His Firm:

- Restructured the firm's organizational and reporting structures
- Overhauled attorney compensation packages multiple times to ease them toward a structure that aligned with firm goals
- Held attorneys accountable to production goals and terminated underperforming attorneys
- Turned over the entire marketing department
- Got very granular on the data and ROI of marketing efforts
- Fired the person doing his accounting and hired a professional, in-house accountant
- Made a significant investment in a COO who systematized and documented everything
- Terminated that COO when he was no longer the right fit for the firm
- Made hiring the right people the focus and refused to compromise
- Spread the culture throughout the entire firm
- Invested heavily in outside consultants:
  - CFO
  - Culture
  - Mindset

Quotes from Sebastian:

"Feedback is a gift — you aren't going to hurt me with it. Having the feedback and the truth from somebody who is not part of the firm is invaluable."

"You need somebody to hold up a mirror. If you don't like what you see — don't blame the mirror. Look at what's true. Show me what's wrong, and I'll go fix it. The truth won't hurt my feelings; losing hurts my feelings."

"A good lawyer isn't necessarily good for your business."

"If we are going to be the best, we are going to have to innovate. Some of these initiatives are going to fail. Fail forward."

"I was learning new things. I found that some people weren't going to change, so they had to go."

"I offloaded jobs as soon as I could afford to. The things I wasn't great at, I couldn't learn fast enough, so it wasn't worth trying to learn."

"Winning is a very dirty process. I got really good at the Red Wedding (terminating people)."

PART 4

THE SALES PROCESS

IN DECEMBER 2013, Chris walked into his son-in-law's office, sat down in a chair, and said, "I'm getting out. Either I can sell the firm to you, or I can shut down, and you can go find somewhere else to work."

Tim, who had been working for Chris for about five years, responded, "Right now?"

Chris replied, "Yeah, right now."

Having never worked anywhere else and knowing that the firm had a good inventory of cases, he said, "OK, I'll buy it." Unfortunately, that response started five years of resentment, frustration, sleepless nights, panic, and desperation for Tim.

The reason Tim believes his father-in-law sold the firm was that he had made enough money to retire, and he had some personal things to take care of that he couldn't do while running the firm. Within a month of that conversation, Chris left his wife. Within a year, he remarried. And within two years, his then-ex-wife died.

On the plus side, Chris had trained Tim and knew he could handle all the cases they had in inventory. It had been a pretty run-of-the-mill personal injury firm for most of Chris' career, with just one other attorney in the office. But when a federal magistrate joined the firm in 2006, cases and overhead exploded. By the time Tim joined, there were seven attorneys handling very complex cases. And in retrospect, Tim thinks Chris was probably struggling to run a firm that had morphed drastically so late in his career.

On December 31st, Chris and Tim signed the papers. It only took a couple of weeks, and Tim had pretty much gone along with whatever Chris suggested — he was his father-in-law, after all. Tim believes Chris had a number in his head of what the firm was worth (probably about five million) based on the cases they already had. They came up with the following deal structure:

- For the first three years, seller receives one-third of all revenue
- For the next two years, seller receives fifteen percent of revenue
- Seller loans buyer $20,000
- Seller cosigns a line of credit for $250,000

On January 1st, Tim began to understand what he had done the day before, and panic set in.

Tim realized that he had agreed to grant one-third of every fee to Chris and one-third went to the referring attorney (because all his cases come through referrals). This meant that he had to run his firm and live on the remaining one-third. He knew the only way he could pay his father-in-law back and avoid bankruptcy was to win all the cases. And win them big. Luckily, he is a personal injury attorney, so that was an option.

If Tim and Chris had used professionals to help with the sale, Tim would not have ended up in his situation. Both parties would have received advice on fair pricing and good terms. The pace of the deal would have at least meant that the line of credit was ready, and Tim would have known what was in store for him when taking on this new challenge.

Selling your firm is a once-in-a-lifetime event. Being able to understand the process and knowing which professionals to rely on can translate not only to more money but also to your peace of mind.

CHAPTER 17

HIRE PROFESSIONALS

The man who represents himself
has a fool for a client.

—ABRAHAM LINCOLN

TIM'S EXPERIENCE WAS very different than my client Sheryle, who bought her firm through a broker. The lack of outside advisors with in-depth knowledge cost Tim an immense amount of money (and mental anguish). Tim's deal was not made out of spite or greed. It was just simple ignorance on the part of both sides. Was it a completely bad deal? Well, it certainly didn't have any limits on it, which generally isn't a good idea. And if a professional had looked at it, they would have said there is no way you can run a profitable firm on 33 percent of revenue.

Whether you are buying or selling, when you get to the actual deal, emotions start to run high, insecurities surface (especially on the part of the seller), and frustrations can easily boil over. Building the right team to support you through the process makes an enormous difference. They'll work with you to ensure you have a successful exit rather than one where both parties are left with regrets, bruised egos, and hurt feelings. It is hard to successfully transition a firm from one owner to the next when your blood boils every time you see each other, which might be every day for the next six to eighteen months.

Who do you need on your team? It's quite a list and includes:

- Broker
- Valuation expert or appraiser
- Forensic accountant
- Tax advisor
- Transactional attorney
- Ethics attorney
- Banker

But more important than all of these team members is deciding who your go-to person will be. Who are you going to rely on when you are frustrated? Who can talk you off the ledge? This person could be one of the professionals listed above, or it could be a friend or loved one. But there are two necessary qualifications:

- They must be willing to be honest with you at all times.
- They must have either gone through this process themselves or been through it with their clients.

By going through this, I mean selling a law firm. In a pinch, it can be somebody who sold another professional services company. Essentially, the person needs to be able to tell you what to expect, what is normal, and what to do when things are either going off the rails or going well. Who is going to be your trusted advisor? Once you identify the person who is going to keep you grounded, we can get started on building your deal team.

BUSINESS BROKER

There are lots of business brokers in the world. I'm sure you have seen ads for them and have met them in your networking groups. They all say the same thing: All businesses are the same. If you can sell one, you can sell any of them.

I'm here to tell you that is categorically NOT TRUE. Professional services are different than most other companies as they are not asset-based. What does that mean? Most businesses own machinery that can be sold, inventory that can be unloaded, work in progress (WIP) that can be completed and monetized, and receivables that can be collected. All of these have value and are used to secure debt. Business brokers understand these types of companies.

Your law firm owns no equipment beyond some computers that were obsolete within weeks of buying them. Inventory? Nope. WIP? Yes, you have WIP. You have unbilled time, but not just anybody can complete that work. And receivables? Now we are getting into a gray area — if a bank foreclosed on a loan secured by the receivables of a law firm, could they actually collect the receivables, or would that be fee sharing?

Yes. Lawyers are special and don't fit the mold. That is why it is so important to have a business broker who specializes in representing law firms. If you can't find one of those, at the very least, look for one who consistently works with accountants. By the way, dentists and most doctors are different from your type of practice because they usually have a bunch of valuable equipment.

Brokers who work exclusively, or at least extensively, in the legal industry also have contacts that can be very helpful. They can direct you to obscure providers when problems come up with a deal, and their reputations in the legal industry can help attract buyers.

When Sheryle told me the law firm she was interested in purchasing was being offered by Tom Lenfestey of The Law Practice Exchange, I was relieved. Tom and his team meet all of the above requirements. They have been at this for over ten years, and one of the things I like most about him is his focus on the deal itself. He is less of a seller's broker and more of a representative for the deal. He wants a deal that works for both sides. He works to make deals fair for both sides and wants them to go as smoothly as possible for both sides. When using Tom's group, each side rarely needs its own brokers.

TRANSACTION ATTORNEY

If you think you can get this done yourself, please reread the quote at the beginning of this chapter. Otherwise, are you a transactional attorney who specializes in transitional-based sales of professional services firms? You're not? I didn't think so.

A lot of people think this is like a real estate closing. It's not. We are talking about a contract with a lot of ins and outs that brings in topics that don't tend to be favorites and strong suits of a lot of attorneys. I'm talking about financials here.

This is a financial transaction, and every adjustment made to the deal will have an impact on another area. Your attorney should be able to understand and anticipate what those repercussions will be and explain them to you so you can make informed decisions. A lot of people ask me if that's not the job of the broker. And yes, it is. But you also want your attorney to understand the transaction and be able to make sure they agree with what the broker is saying.

A few checks and balances now will save you a lot of headaches down the line. Your broker is not an attorney and will never catch the little things in the contract that can cause such huge headaches later.

VALUATION EXPERT

The valuation expert or appraiser does precisely what the role suggests: they help find the value of the business. The seller will often come to the table having already had the firm valued. And that value will probably be to their advantage. The buyer can also have their own valuation done. And inevitably, it will be done to their advantage. At this point, the haggling starts. As long as the final price is supported by the numbers, it's fine.

Does every deal need a high-priced, professionally done valuation? No. If you are dealing with a reputable broker and can agree on a multiple, then it is a simple math formula to get to the "number." Is a valuation helpful as a starting point? Absolutely.

Tim's situation should be a cautionary tale. While he was able to make the payments necessary to pay off his father-in-law, they were onerous. One of the things that The Law Practice Exchange focuses on is whether the firm will be able to service the debt created by the sale. In Tim's case, Tom would have said it would not. Having an outside person with no allegiance to either party can ensure a deal that works for both parties.

TAX ACCOUNTANT

The tax accountant is more for the seller than the buyer, but nonetheless, they are important. There are various ways to structure the deal, and that can have big tax implications. Being tax efficient is important, and you can't leave this to be figured out at the signing table. Make sure your accountant is brought into the conversation when you *decide* to sell so any changes to corporate structure that need to be made can be done early enough. Not having a tax accountant on your team can cost you an immense amount come April 15th.

FORENSIC ACCOUNTANT

While the tax accountant is mostly for the seller, accountants are important for both sides. When they decide to sell, the seller needs a good accountant to come on board to clean up the books and ensure they are ready for inspection. The buyer needs a forensic accountant to carry out that inspection. Buyers definitely don't want to find out post-deal that the firm they bought is not what was represented.

Accountants for both sides need audit experience and the ability to dig deep to understand complex transactions and to follow trails to ensure the books are as clean as possible.

BANKER

Most people think they have the banker covered, but few do. SBA (U.S. Small Business Administration) is the best resource for financing the purchase of law firms. Most banks do SBA loans, but again, law firms aren't normal companies, and banks are used to lending based on assets. You don't have any, at least not any physical ones the lender can come take and then turn around and sell if you default on the loan.

There are a few banks that specialize in professional service loans with the SBA. Do your research and make sure you are working with one that has extensive experience lending to companies without tangible assets. Interview them and ask how many of these sales they have done. Ask how long it takes to get the loan done and ask specifics about what they are going to need. Getting this information at the outset makes it less likely you'll have surprises later on.

I heard a story recently of a firm that ignored this advice and worked with their local bank, which assured them they had lots of SBA experience and could do the loan. They started their due diligence, and the bank asked for information. Then, they said they needed more information, which, of course, cost money. Then, the bank needed something else that required a professional to produce a report, which incurred more fees. All in all, it took six months and a ton of fees for the buyer.

At this point, most people look at me and say, "Isn't that normal?" And the answer is, "No, it's not." If you are working with a law firm vertical lender, an SBA loan should take about sixty days, and the fees should be fairly low. Over a certain dollar amount, a site visit is required — even if you have a virtual firm and that "site" is your kitchen table.

Many people want to use their existing bank, such as Bank of America, Chase, PNC, or even Truist. This is an option if you don't qualify for an SBA loan, but realistically, the only financing they will give you is credit based on your existing firm. Your odds of receiving a loan go up in direct proportion to your trust account balance. These banks don't have the specialized knowledge necessary to loan to non-asset-based businesses. The same can be said for credit unions. They were built for car and house loans — and if they can't repo it, they don't want to lend on it!

There is one other lender that is available almost exclusively to personal injury firms, and that is private equity. These firms understand the risks inherent in personal injury firms. They understand their business model and can look at the case inventory and easily calculate the revenue that will come in over the next twelve to thirty-six months.

You will pay the price for that money — it will be the most expensive option of the ones we've discussed. But it is an option. Unfortunately, at the moment, private equity is not very interested in other practice areas.

ESTATE PLANNING ATTORNEY

For some people, selling their firm has an impact on their estate plans. Think back to Sebastian's father in the last section. Because they did not plan ahead, Sebastian and his dad are currently trying to play catchup and find creative (but legal) ways to avoid a large estate tax bill.

FINANCIAL PLANNER

If you are selling your firm, you should know your "number." The one that, after taxes, will allow you to not only feel good about the sale but also contribute mightily toward your financial stability. A financial planner is a person who needs to enter your life at the beginning of this process to help you set attainable goals.

These professionals are the people who will guide you through the uncharted waters of your deal. Bringing them on early, even before you "officially" decide to sell, allows you to get to know them. It is easier to take advice from somebody you know, like, and trust in the high-stress times of selling your firm.

Because Sheryle found the firm she bought cruising the internet on a Sunday afternoon as opposed to during an intentional search, she had very few of these people set up. I got a call not long after she started due diligence, and she was a little unnerved. She sent the financials to her accountants to see what they thought, and the response she got was, "Looks good." While she wasn't sure what she wanted, she knew she wanted more than that.

She sent the information to her tax accountant, looking for two things: a valuation from a valuation expert and due diligence/audit work from a forensic accountant. Her tax accountant was not qualified to do either. She was setting him up for failure and, by extension, herself as well. It was at this point that we started building a team to help her through the process.

SUMMARY

Attorneys are smart people. They've studied different practice areas in law school and, throughout their careers, have worked with many other professions. For these reasons, many feel like they can save a little money and do the deal on their own. However, it's important to remember that just like you are an expert in your particular field of law, other professionals are experts in their fields. Lean on them. They have been through this before. Use their experience to make your transaction smoother and less stressful.

To get started assembling your team, go to **ExitOnTopBook.com** where you'll find a list of recommended professionals and resources.

CHAPTER 18

THE TRANSACTION

ATTORNEYS ARE TRAINED to know every step of a process and every potential outcome before they take any kind of action. In most cases, the parties entering into a sale are both first timers. As a result, personal experience is scarce. People rely on friends who have had experiences that might not be relevant, and emotions tend to run high. This is why your team of professionals is so important. They have been there, done that, and know what is going to happen. Lean on them for advice and listen when they tell you to get out of the middle of something. An emotional seller is never beneficial to a deal.

Every firm sale follows a general path. However, each one is individual, and as the seller, you need to trust both your broker and the process, so don't wait to start building your team.

Here are the basic steps in selling your firm:

- Listing the firm
- Meeting potential buyers
- Due diligence
- Financing
- Closing
- Transition

LISTING THE FIRM

Once you have optimized your firm, it is time to find the right broker and get the process started. Before listing it, your broker will want to know what you want to get out of the sale. Basically, they will start where this book started. What are your goals and your hopes? And yes, they will ask what price you want. There will be a discussion about nonnegotiables. Hopefully, they will give you some guidance on what is and is not realistic, and they will help you crystalize what is most important.

Once they know where you want to go, your broker is going to look under the hood to understand how your firm runs and to gain a working knowledge of the firm so they can sell it. They will look not only at how the firm operates but also at the results of those operations — your financials. While brokers want to show every firm in a positive light, they need to know where problems exist since they have to be honest with potential buyers (the equivalent of the "seller's disclosure" in a real estate transaction). The upside of this intensive review is that when they find issues, they're also ready to offer solutions to fix problems and/or help them appear less significant.

Once the broker has a complete picture of the firm, they will come back to you to discuss expectations. The most important one is price. You might want to get $1.5 million for the firm, but if the broker, who may have brought in a valuation expert at this point, can't justify that price or make the numbers work, you might need to accept that you aren't going to get it. At this point, you have a choice to make. Do you want to stop the process and fix the things that will increase the value, or would you rather sell for a lower price?

There will be other discussions about your nonnegotiables — again with the goal of adjusting expectations. If you want to limit the geographic area of the buyer, that is going to affect the timeline. You have cut out a lot of potential buyers, and it will be harder to find someone. If you want to sell quickly, it will probably affect the price. This is the time to go back to your nonnegotiables list, discuss it with your broker, and understand how things will impact the transaction.

MEETING POTENTIAL BUYERS

Your firm has been prepped for sale, and now it's time to meet potential buyers. Your broker has gone out, teased your firm, and gotten some people who want more information since any ads will have little or no identifiable information. This is when you hand over that deal killer letter and start weeding out the people who aren't a "Yes." Remember, the goal is to get to "No" as fast as possible so you don't waste time. If you still don't have your deal killer letter, go to ExitOnTopBook.com for help.

At some point, you will find somebody who says, "Yes." They think your nonnegotiables, including price, are reasonable. They like the sound of your firm, and in theory, you have a verbal deal, so it's time for them to dig deep. It's time for due diligence.

DUE DILIGENCE

I once had a client who called me and was very annoyed. He was selling part of his firm, and the buyer had sent over a due diligence list. He was outraged they were ... Well, I can't say it here. Let's just say he felt his hindquarters were being invaded. When I saw the list, I tried my best not to laugh. It was about six questions, and the one he objected to the most was "Three Years of Financials."

Unfortunately, the reaction that particular client had is pretty common, but buyers have questions. The first two things they'll want to know initially are:

- Is the firm profitable?
- Where do the clients come from?

To get those answers, they are going to dig around in your firm and ask a lot of questions. And it is not a quid pro quo situation. You don't get to ask any of the same questions in return. So yes, it is very one-sided, but this is part of the process of selling.

Focus on your goals. What are you getting out of this? What is your life going to look like post-sale? Don't be afraid to talk with your broker or your go-to person about your feelings. They have likely seen it before and can help you through the process.

Is the Firm Profitable?

To answer this question, a buyer looks to your financials. They're going to want, at the very least, your profit and loss statement and balance sheet from the last three years. Depending on how long ago COVID was, they might ask for five. Once they have given these a look, they will continue to dig deeper. Expect to turn over firm tax filings and potentially even let their financial people dig around in your actual QuickBooks files. Invasive? Yes. But remember, you are selling to them, and they need to feel confident that what you have represented is what they are actually buying.

Where Do Clients Come From?

While a law firm has many parts that add value to the firm, if it doesn't have clients, it won't have revenue. No revenue means no value. A buyer is going to want to see the data that shows how clients come to the firm to ensure that when you sell it, the new client flow won't stop.

This is where that technology we talked about can make such a difference. No buyer wants a seller that just shrugs their shoulders and says, "I don't know. Clients just keep showing up." They want a seller who shows up, hands them reports, and starts explaining which marketing generates which clients, how much it costs, how they track it, and how they make decisions about which marketing to start, stop, or continue. That makes their little buyer hearts beat just a bit faster.

FINANCING

While due diligence is happening, the buyer is also off arranging financing. Depending on whether or not you are willing to finance part of the sales price, this may or may not include you.

If you are not financing any of it, the buyer will work with their banker to secure a loan. As previously discussed, this can take anywhere from sixty days to six months. If they have the cash, it can go much faster.

If you are financing part of the sale, you do get to "look under their skirt" a little. You can run a credit report on them to see if you think they are a good credit risk. But no, you don't get to go through their financials with a fine-tooth comb like they are doing to yours. Sorry.

CLOSING

This is the stage you have both been waiting for. Just like with any closing, it involves lots of signatures, lots of paperwork, and a deposit in the bank.

In most cases, it can feel slightly anticlimactic because you still have to show up for work the next day. Rarely does an attorney sell and walk away from the firm on the same day. It is not the nature of our very relationship-driven businesses. You still have to stay and complete the transition.

TRANSITION

In a well-planned sale, the transition begins way back during the due diligence process. As the seller, you may have decades of institutional knowledge to pass on to the new owner in whatever amount of time was negotiated. Additionally, it's likely that at least one of the parties is a first-time buyer or seller, and there is additional stress around the process because of the unknown nature of the experience. None of this bodes well for the relationship.

A best-practice strategy is to set up a weekly transition meeting. It can be a formal meeting or a casual lunch — that is up to the two of you. The important thing is that you have a regular meeting cadence where you build the trust needed to carry you through the transaction and transition. This also provides a scheduled opportunity to bring up and address issues as they occur.

I recently heard a story about a broker who checked in with a buyer a few months after the close to see how things were going. He was told that business was down, and the buyer was concerned. The broker then asked how many meetings the seller had set up with major clients and referral partners to transition those relations. The answer was none.

The broker called the seller, who sat in the office right next door to the buyer, and asked how things were going, pointing out that he was aware that revenue was down. The seller replied, "Yeah, I know. I keep waiting for him to ask me to set up meetings with all my referral sources, but he hasn't come to me yet."

Avoid these types of miscommunications by starting the transition long before you close the deal. Talk about everything that is going on in the firm. If revenue is down, talk about why and look for solutions together. If there is a problem in marketing, you (as the seller) are likely to have a fair amount of institutional knowledge to offer. However, it's a good idea to meet with the buyer to tap their expertise for potential new ideas. Rarely does a seller walk away with all their money on closing day, so welcome the new ideas.

The person who bought Mike's niche law firm has done some amazing things. She has almost doubled the size of the firm in the first year. Since Mike gets between 6 percent and 10 percent of revenue (based on pre-established targets), he benefits from all the improvements, and as a result, he's going to end up getting much more than his original sales price. The transition is a partnership. It might be a short one, but you both have an interest in making it as successful as possible.

SUMMARY

I'm not going to say there are no shortcuts in the transaction process. There certainly are, and you can take them. Chris did it when he sold his firm to Tim, but look how it turned out for Tim — not so great. The process exists for a reason. Start by building your team. While transactions aren't fast, if you plan each step and effectively execute the plan, both you and the buyer are likely to close a deal that makes you both happy — and, hopefully, a few bags of money for you!

CHAPTER 19

WHAT TO EXPECT

I OFTEN TALK about partnerships as business marriages. The transaction is a short-term partnership with a timer on it, so maybe it isn't quite like a marriage. Maybe it is closer to your first boyfriend or girlfriend — short-term, high drama, emotional, and destined to end. But the goal is for it to end with everybody walking away feeling good.

How do you do that? You go back to part 1 of this book and remember how you answered these questions: How do you define success? What do you want out of this process? What are your nonnegotiables?

Keep these answers front and center as you go through the process, and it will allow you to stay strong.

The hardest thing about selling your firm, after you have it running really well and very profitably, is managing your expectations. You need to work with your broker to understand what a realistic price is and to know where to compromise (or not) on the deal's other terms.

When a final deal is set, you won't be able to walk away from your firm at the closing table. You will have to continue working for at least six months and up to two years. Transitions like these take effort and are built on trust and open communication. The faster this platform is built, the more successful the two of you will be.

Chances are high that you will have to finance part of the purchase price. The buyer might not be able to get enough financing, and they might want to incentivize you to make the transition a good one. Don't be afraid of this. It certainly worked in Mike's favor.

It is easy to feel overwhelmed. The buyer is going to request information you probably don't think they have a right to see, and you don't get to ask for anything in return. It will feel one-sided. And the requests will keep coming while you are still trying to run your firm. Take a deep breath. Talk to your broker to ensure they aren't making unreasonable demands (it just feels like they are), and realize that this process takes time. And remember — you don't have to return information the day it is requested.

Finally, trust your professionals. They have all done this before and are there to ensure the deal goes smoothly. Stay out of their way and let them do their jobs. Yes, you went to law school, but this is the first time you have sold a firm, so don't micromanage and try to draft the contracts. Anytime the owner gets involved in these kinds of details, it slows the deal down. I know somebody who did a number of acquisitions, and when she went to buy a company, she would insist the owner move their office out of the building. Otherwise, they would get in the way and muck up the process.

You won't know exactly what is going to happen next, and you probably won't be able to control it. What you can control is the ultimate outcome, and that's all that matters. Focus on what comes after the sale, and the rest will work itself out.

TIM'S CASE STUDY

Chris, Tim's father-in-law, decided, seemingly on a whim, to sell the firm. They did not use outside advisors. Chris pushed the sale through in a matter of weeks, and Tim was left with a deal that almost crushed him financially for five years. This is a real-life cautionary tale of what happens when two attorneys think they don't need professionals.

Revenue	$2.5MM		
Net Income	$820K		
SDE	$940K		
Price	Supported	Intended	Actual
Multiple of SDE	2.5	3.5X	11.7X
Sales Price	$2.35MM	$3.25MM	$11.0MM
Type of Buyer	Owner Operator – Family		

Why the Firm Should Have Been Valued Lower:

- The firm had no website.
- There was no marketing of any kind.
- There was no filing system. Tim had to take the firm paperless.

- The associates were not stable and did not stay with the firm.

Why Chris Thought It Had Value:

- Since it was a personal injury practice, he knew what cases were in inventory and could estimate what he thought they would settle for over the next three years.
- He knew that Tim was a talented attorney who would do good work.
- He had faith in Tim's ability to keep the firm afloat and pay off the deal as structured.

How Tim Made the Deal Work:

- He educated himself as a lawyer:
  - Attended as many seminars on negotiation as he could find
  - Attended trial academies and seminars
  - Hired experts where necessary
- He increased the average settlements and jury awards by a factor of almost 10X. He knew that if he only had one-third to run the firm and live on, it had to be a big one-third.

CONCLUSION

I STARTED THIS book talking about why you wanted to sell and what was next. And I want to go back to that. Focusing on who you are going to be and what you are going to be able to do once this transaction is over is what will carry you through this process. And I use the word process very specifically.

To successfully sell your firm, you need to walk through a process:

- Map out life after law
- Understand where the value is in your firm
- Decide what needs to be fixed in the firm
- Make changes
- Sell the firm

The problem for any attorney with a process is analysis paralysis. Many times, they will spend years thinking about selling, researching, reading, looking at articles, and talking to people but not taking any action. When they do eventually take action, their timeline is too short to be able to affect their sale price, and they find themselves in a fire sale.

Selling your firm starts three to five years before you *think* you might want to do it. So start now. Do it today. And here's a little secret — you don't have to figure out your life after law to start creating a saleable firm. Start by analyzing the firm to figure out where you could increase its value and do that. You are never obligated to sell.

And then, when you think you might be ready, start to look ahead to life after law. What do you want to do next? Who are you going to be? Where will you live? How will you spend your day? And it better be something you are excited about.

Why? Because I want you running, not walking, toward that future.

THANK YOU

AT CATHCAP, we are a bunch of numbers people who can read your financials like a book. While that enables us to see everything that is happening in a firm, it certainly does not enable us to fix it. I have spoken with authority in this book about topics well out of my wheelhouse, and it was only possible by relying on the expertise and generosity of others.

Sunny Lowe has always believed in giving back. I first met him years ago at a weekly pitch meeting called 1 Million Cups. As I was working on this book, he came to one of our EO meetings and talked about how he had sold his company. It was perfect timing as I was just starting to write the book, and everything he said was hitting home. He generously agreed to lunch and really shaped the sections on nonnegotiables and the deal killer letter.

Nanda Grandison from yorCMO helped immensely with the marketing section. I found Nanda when I realized that Cathcap needed to hire strategic advice that drives profit — just in marketing. Fellow EO'er Joe Frost owns yorCMO, and when he connected us with Nanda, it was

187

like finding our equivalent, just in a different vertical. She not only advised on the book but has also done incredible things to move our business forward.

I first met Kerri Coby White at a conference, where she was one of the only other females in a sea of men — and then I saw her on a panel on stage. She is a go-to expert when it comes to intake — especially for personal injury. She taught me about the need for empathy and how easy it is for the intake team to become numb to the tragedy they hear every day. Of course, we at Cathcap also like Kerri and her company because they are data-driven.

Tom Lenfestey from The Law Practice Exchange is invaluable anytime anything deal-related comes up. He can be counted on to always have the right contact and know the right answer. He is beyond generous with his time. Tom wants nothing more than for lawyers to be able to sell the firms they have worked a lifetime building and realize the value they have created.

And a special shoutout to all the clients who agreed to share even more about buying and selling their firms with me. I withheld their names because the information is so sensitive, yet they shared everything with me — their financials and their fears. But more than anything, I am grateful they allowed Cathcap on the ride to grow their firms.

ABOUT THE AUTHOR

BROOKE DISCOVERED HER passion for helping entrepreneurial lawyers build their firms by working with her father. After getting her MBA in corporate finance and investments at Texas Christian University and a quick stint at a hedge fund, she found herself helping her family establish a new firm, which hit the seven-figure mark within eighteen months. Soon thereafter, she started talking to other lawyers who asked, "Can you do for us what you do for your family?"

This is when Brooke realized that most attorneys don't run their firms by the numbers. They are making decisions based on their gut, and that causes a lot of anxiety — not to mention a loss of profitability. With that insight, Brooke started Cathcap, a fractional CFO company designed to maximize law firm profitability.

Since 2013, Brooke and her team have helped hundreds of firms make data-driven decisions to drive faster growth and more predictability in their businesses. As a CFO, Brooke looks at every part of a firm that touches the money — and that's the whole firm. This eventually led her to become an EOS Implementer®. Through EOS, Brooke helps firms gain clarity on their vision, discipline, and accountability to increase traction and develop a healthy, functional leadership team.

Brooke weaves the technical knowledge from her MBA with her real-world experience to create speeches that have entertained groups worldwide, such as Entrepreneur's Organization, bar associations, and conferences like PILMMA Super Summit, 360 Advocacy, and the Louisiana Association of Justice. She has written numerous books, including her international best-selling series *From Panic to Profit*™. Brooke has been featured in *Forbes*, *US News and World Report*, and on CNBC. She also has a monthly financial column in *Attorney at Work* and is frequently requested as a podcast guest.

Brooke can be reached at Brooke@cathcap.com.

www.ingramcontent.com/pod-product-compliance
Lightning Source LLC
Chambersburg PA
CBHW071605210326
41597CB00019B/3408